Biddulph

within living memory

Phoebe and Ernest Nixon on their Diamond Wedding Anniversary, 1960.

Compiled by Bill Ridgway

Cover: 'Under-the-Hill' by C.W. Brown
Courtesy of the Potteries Museum & Art Gallery. Stoke on Trent
Back cover: The Rev Fletcher with Messrs Brown, Beech (G and H), Plant, Hall, Finney, Nixon and Lancaster on Bailey's Hill in celebration of George V's Silver Jubilee, 1935.

For the people of Biddulph Moor
and their children

'Under-the-Hill' by C.W. Brown
Courtesy of the Potteries Museum & Art Gallery. Stoke on Trent

CHURNET VALLEY BOOKS
1 King Street, Leek, Staffordshire. ST13 5NW 01538 399033
www.leekbooks.co.uk

ISBN 1 904546 25 0

Acknowledgements

In writing this book I would like to acknowledge the help I've received from the people of Biddulph Moor, who welcomed me into their homes, loaned me their photographs and shared their reminiscences unfazed either by my temperamental tape-recorder or the endless questions I put to them. Apart from the interviewees listed below, I'd like to thank Mrs Susan Mayes, Headteacher of Moor First School, for allowing me to intrude into her busy day by granting me access to the school logs and other material relevant to the history of the village, the Rev Peter Toon, former Rector of Christ Church, for indulging my passion for church archives, and the staff of Biddulph library for putting up with my constant requests for information without obvious signs of stress. Finally, I wish to express my gratitude to those involved in the production of Hill Top and New Road Methodist Church Anniversary booklets, to Jim Nixon for his autobiographical 'A Brief History of My Life', and to Ailsa Booth for her copious notes and jottings - and for introducing me to 'My Childhood Memories on the Moor' by the late Annie Cook. All these I have read with pleasure and I extend thanks to those who have allowed me to make use of extracts in this book.

My interviewees were:

Ewart Nixon (b.1930). Ewart gave me a general picture of Biddulph Moor in his lifetime, and from the start helped clarify the areas of village life which would form a useful basis for this book.

Ailsa Booth (b.1920). Ailsa produced a compendium of dates, facts and figures gleaned from personal reminiscences, scraps, photos and cuttings. Her long service as secretary to Biddulph Moor School proved invaluable to the project.

Jane Doorbar (b.1912). Jane provided me with a valuable insight into the village at the end of the Great War and throughout the 1920s, and furnished me with many details regarding the origin of Primitive Methodism in the area.

Jim Nixon (b.1920). Jim's account of farming, particularly between the wars and during WW2, was both informative and enlightening, and if he was surprised at the extent of my ignorance, he never let it show.

Anne Newton (b.1944). Tommy Fletcher (b.1917). Anne and her uncle Tommy told me much about the musical activities of the village and the development of the nationally acclaimed Greenway Moor Prize Band.

Malcolm Locker (b.1928). Malcolm, who taught on Biddulph Moor from 1954 to 1958, imparted a wealth of information about his time working with Headmaster Smith Holmes.

Elsie Evans (b.1924). Elsie furnished me with abundant information regarding the working day at Bailey's Shirt Factory before and during the War.

Lillian Armitt (b.1922). As Senior Dining Room Supervisor at 'Top' School 1952-71, Lillian complemented Malcolm's account of the school and threw light on the changing provision of school meals over two decades.

Clarice Boon (b. 1921). In her role as District Nurse and midwife, Clarice filled the gaps in my knowledge of medical provision in the area in the early Fifties.

Marian Flynn (b.1931). Marian's lifetime connection with the New Road Wesleyan Chapel meant she was well-placed to explain the influence of Methodism on Biddulph Moor, and the part played by her family in its development.

Phyllis and Harold Nixon (b.1926/1924 respectively). Phyllis and Harold enlivened my ear with their anecdotes relating to their time as shopkeepers on the moor.

Arthur Barlow (b.1925). Although based in Biddulph, Arthur's police duties brought him into contact with Biddulph Moor. He provided a good insight into his years on the beat (1949-54) and the day-to-day activities of the local force.

Robert and Agnes Pass (b.1926 and 1926). Bob's experiences as right-hand man to undertaker Billy Booth and the Revs Fletcher and Withington, successive Rectors of Christ Church, was recounted with gentle humour and a sharp insight into the characters of all three, while his wife Agnes remembered her schooldays.

Ken and Mary Pointon (b.1928 and 1935). Ken and Mary recounted the history of the fustian throughout the war and into the early fifties. Ex-bandsman Ken couldn't resist further anecdotes about the Greenway Moor Prize Band, while they both contributed to my knowledge of local mining and of Christ Church.

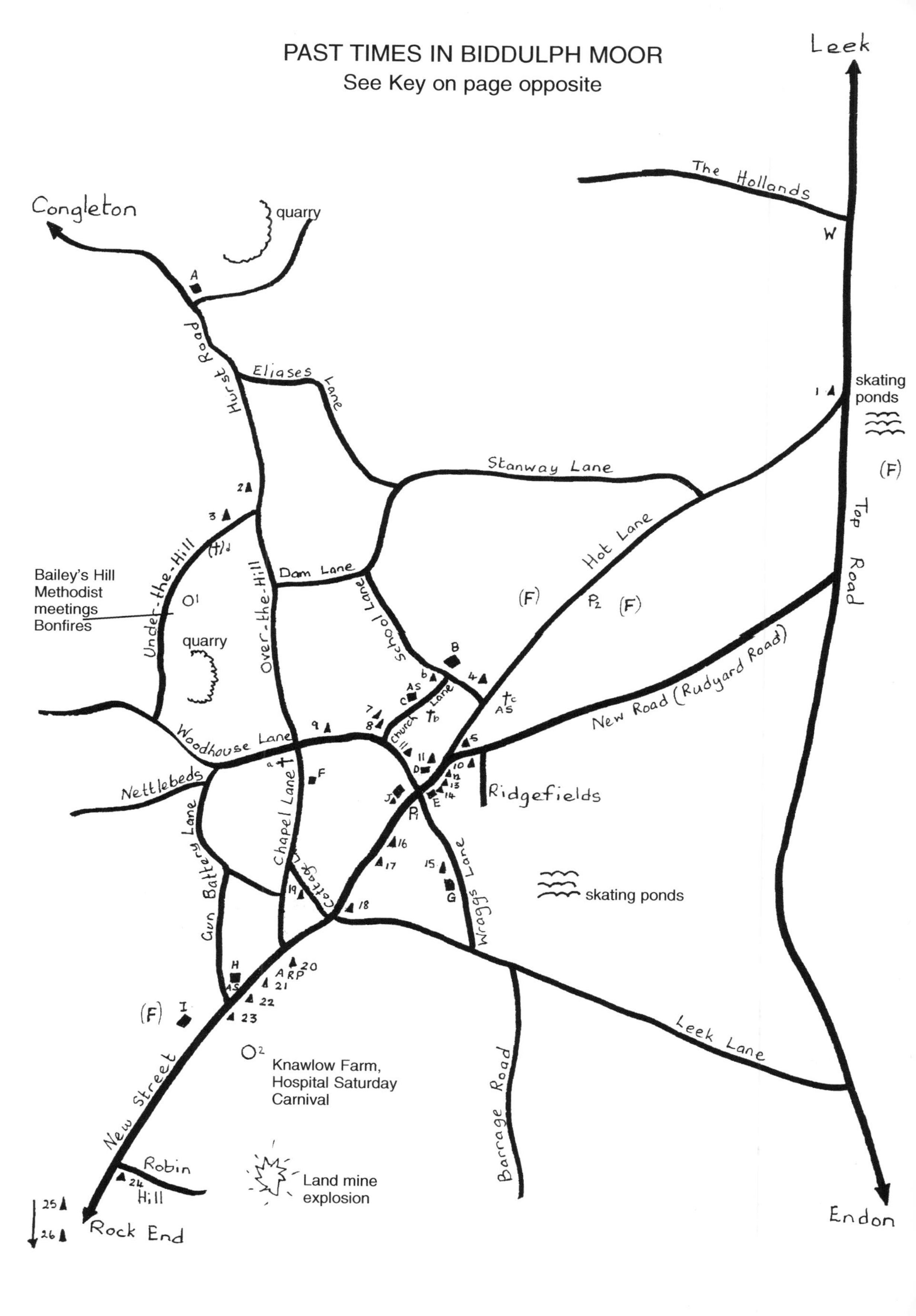
PAST TIMES IN BIDDULPH MOOR
See Key on page opposite
Leek
The Hollands
W
Congleton
quarry
A
Hurst Road
Eliases Lane
skating ponds
Stanway Lane
(F)
Top Road
Hot Lane
Under-the-Hill
Over-the-Hill
Dam Lane
School Lane
Bailey's Hill Methodist meetings Bonfires
quarry
(F)
P2
(F)
B
New Road (Rudyard Road)
Church Lane
Woodhouse Lane
Nettlebeds
Chapel Lane
Ridgefields
Gun Battery Lane
Cottage Lane
Wraggs Lane
skating ponds
H
I
(F)
O2
Knawlow Farm, Hospital Saturday Carnival
Leek Lane
Barrage Road
New Street
Robin Hill
Land mine explosion
Rock End
Endon

Contents

OPPOSITE PAGE: PLAN OF BIDDULPH MOOR: KEY BELOW

▲ Shops and trade

1 Royal Shop general store
2 Beech's Store, Hurst Road
3 Proctor's, agricultural merchants
4 Stanway's, cobblers
5 Booth's, undertakers, joinery
6 School tuckshop
7/8 Brown's and Beech's: haberdashery, shoes, cobbler's
9 Shufflebotham's: petrol, furniture, coal
10 Polly Lovatt's general store
11 New Road: Clem Simpson, butcher, later footwear (Nixon's)
11 Woodhouse Lane: Nixon's footwear. Also clothing, toys
12 Wilshaw's, clothes
13 Sherratt's Post Office
14 Newton's General Store, later Spar, now Londis
15 Beech's Shoe Repairs, also see 7 above
16 Plant's Yard: variously a butcher's, fish and chip shop, sweet shop, hairdressers
17 Co-op
18 Nixon's: bread, cakes, home-knitted garments
19 Sidney Hulme: Newsagent
20 Gaskill's wool shop
21 Holland's: charged up accumulators, sold batteries
22 Holdcroft's: cobbler's
23 Martha Ann Brown's general store
24 Wood's general store
25 Lovatt's general store
26 Taylor's general store

† Church and Chapel

a Hill Top Methodist Church, 1904
b Christ Church (C of E), 1863
c New Road Methodist Church, 1888
d Under-the-Hill Methodist Chapel (converted to housing)

■ Prominent Buildings

A Spring House, or Hurst Towers, 1872: previous owners include the Holt's and Shadrach Gibson, who saw the potential of the local sand deposits
B Biddulph Moor Council School or Top School, 1908
C Biddulph Moor School, then BM National School, then BM Infants School before becoming Christ Church Hall
D Police station, 1950s
E Police station, 1896
(F) Temporary police station, wartime.
G Bailey's Shirt Factory
H Miners' Welfare, later Hill Top Methodist Hall
I Fustian, then Parr's Paint Factory, then Horton's (furniture). Now Mitras Composites
J Bus Garage and Florrie's General Store. Now Spar
P1 Rose and Crown
P2 New Inn, later the Foxhound

W Searchlight and Lewis gun emplacement, WW2
F Football team practice sites
AS Air raid shelters
ARP Air Raid Patrol headquarters

Bill Ridgway

Bill Ridgway worked in a succession of jobs before gaining a teaching certificate. He later combined a teaching career with educational writing, producing almost 100 books over 30 years. On his retirement from teaching, he wrote monthly articles for the Evening Sentinel publication 'The Way We Were', and became the non-fiction editor for Nelson Thornes. The articles which appeared in 'The Way We Were' were subsequently published as *Potteries Lad* by Churnet Valley. Bill is married with two children and lives in the Staffordshire Moorlands.

The Rev Fletcher with Messrs Brown, Beech (G and H), Plant, Hall, Finney, Nixon and Lancaster on Bailey's Hill in celebration of George V's Silver Jubilee, 1935.

Author's Note

My memory of Biddulph Moor goes back to a chill April day in 1954 when I crested Park Lane and struggled against a stiffening breeze past solitary cottages en route to Rudyard Lake. It was the first time I'd left my home at Chell Heath to venture into 'foreign parts', and it was with some trepidation that I'd earlier packed sandwiches and Dandelion and Burdock into the saddlebag of my second-hand bike and set off into the Great Unknown. I can't remember using a map. I do remember, however, that those first sporadic cottages evolved into a village of smoking chimneys, occasional shops, wooden sheds, a pub on a crossroads and a church. I remember coarse roadside grass clumped with reed, brighter pastures beyond and, quite suddenly, the long upward stretch leading to Top Road.

I cycled through Biddulph Moor many times after that, but always with other destinations in mind. Manifold Valley, Dovedale and Freshwater Pool were among the attractions, and my whetted appetite for adventure soon took me further afield. I was only fourteen, and little guessed that eleven years later I, too, would be living on Biddulph Moor, married and settled in one of the newly-built bungalows mushrooming then throughout the country. At that time, 1965, building had just begun, with the first developments underway in Leek Lane, Rudyard Road and Woodhouse Lane. I was an incomer from the city, as were most of my neighbours. Yet I was soon passing the time of day with Jack Hulme and his brother Frank, sharing musical tastes with Albert who lived just below them, and talking building with Edgar Booth, village stalwarts from a much earlier time. I little realised then that I'd moved into an interdependent community where the same family names had occupied school logs and church registers for more than a century and a half. That alongside Booth and Hulme were Shufflebotham, Nixon, Stanway, Goldstraw, Gibson, Lancaster, Wilshaw, Cotterill, Bailey and a host of other names so numerously similar that even the locals had had to use nicknames to distinguish one family branch from the next. Blueys, Flattens, Pinkies, Slappers, Timothies, Tidleys and Watlers were all Baileys, but you wouldn't find them living at the same address.

Over the forty years I've lived on Biddulph Moor my interest in the area has grown. And as I began to research its history through speaking to villagers whose memories reach back to the early years of the 20th century, a picture has emerged of a rugged, individualistic and self-reliant people who, before the coming of the car and the influx of newcomers like myself, were thrown on to their own resources, provided their own entertainment, played and sang together in bands and choirs and still found time to tend their wheelbarrow farms after a shift at the coal face. The fabric of village life was stitched together through school, church and chapel, through Hospital Saturday and ceremonies to crown the Velvet Queen, through camp meetings and bonfires on Bailey's Hill, through struggling together through ridded roads to Bailey's Shirt Factory or the fustian. Hill Top Church had its first electricity supply in 1935 and its oil lamps were sold a year later, when the village was coupled to mains water and the buckets which until then had made daily journeys to Wright's Well, Trent Well and Gruel Spout were finally hung up. In 1940 the Luftwaffe paid an unexpected visit when a bomber dropped a landmine near Braddow (Bradda) Farm, leaving a sixty foot crater and a lot of work for Jim Nixon, who spent the following day gathering up the only casualties - his dead poultry. Dates such as these define the shared experience of the people, and are a microcosm of a vanished England reflected in the memories of those who lived through them.

But if the coming of electricity, water and German bombers provide a checklist of dates which still linger in the mind, it is the villagers themselves who are at its heart. People like shopkeepers Martha Ann Brown and Sidney 'Times' Hulme; Melodian Joe, entertaining anyone who would listen with an al fresco rendition of 'We Shall Meet on that Beautiful Shore', and bus driver Joe Turner, who reprised his role as Joke Policeman on Hospital Saturdays before the War - names recalled in fondness and in laughter.

It was never my intention to write a cold chronology of village life, and apart from a paragraph or so to provide a context for the various chapters, the narrative is spoken by those whose families have long lived on Biddulph Moor. What I hope has emerged is a glimpse into the simpler, less hurried life of bygone years, and a commitment to keep their memory alive for the sake of all our children.

Bill Ridgway Summer 2005

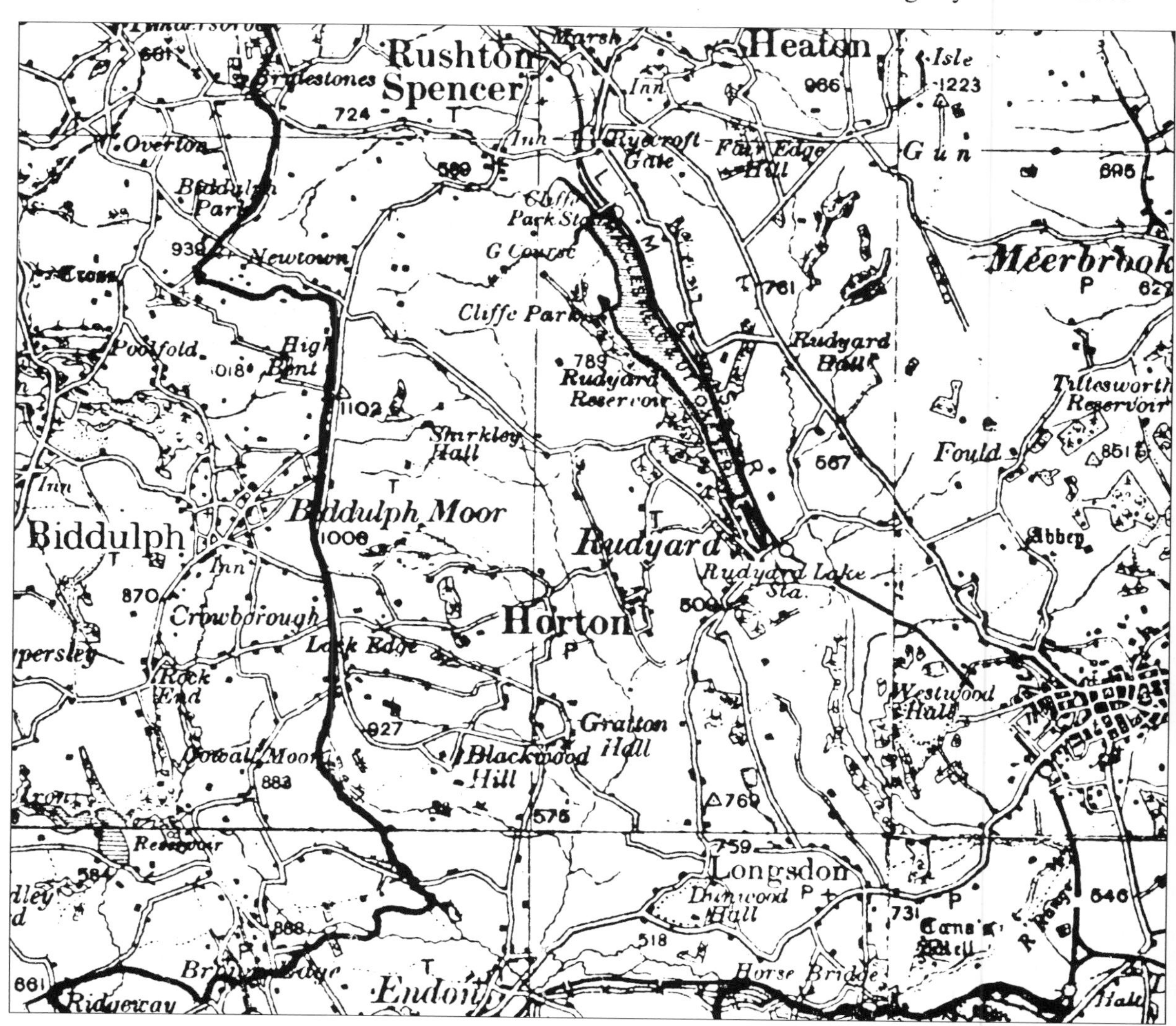

THE MOORLANDS BETWEEN BIDDULPH AND LEEK 1950s.

Chapter 1
Chalk and Talk

"William Bailey says someone has taken his cap. Heather Mayer and Mary Nixon saw Abraham Pass with two caps last night, one on his head and one in his hand. Mistress sent for him this morning. He says that Martha Beech brought one from school and gave it to him. William Bailey and his brother went to Abraham Pass's home, but his mother says he brought no cap home with his own. William Bailey's cap was found later under one of the ventilators of the school."

Christ Church School Log Oct 1873

Biddulph Moor School, now Christ Church Hall, was built by public subscription in 1852, the main benefactor being James Bateman of the Grange. At that time the school comprised the two road-side rooms, one for Infants, the other for mixed classes of older children. The school was to be *'for the children of the labouring, manufacturing and other poorer classes of the Parish'*. Shortage of space led in 1885 to the addition of a large hall, the principal benefactor this time being Robert Heath. The road-side rooms now accommodated the Infants, while the mixed classes occupied the hall. By this time the school had become known as a National School (1870 Education Act).

Continual overcrowding led to the building of the Council School (referred to by the local children as 'Top' School and now Moor First) in 1908. The older children now attended Top School while the Infants remained below.

In 1942, part of the school was requisitioned by the War Office, and the Infants joined the older children in Top School. At the cessation of hostilities the original school became Christ Church Hall, and so it has remained.

At the end of the War, Top School catered for children up to the age of 15. By 1951 it had become a Primary school, and a First School by 1965.

In 1870 the Government made it compulsory to keep School Logs, and Biddulph Moor is particularly fortunate in having a complete set from that date for both schools. Since the names of staff are frequently mentioned in the reminiscences below, it might be useful to record some of the teachers here:

In the case of the Infants School, Margaret Jermyn was principal teacher from 1873 until 1884, when she married Rector Francis Gordon's nephew and left teaching. She was followed by Catherine Dale, who continued as head until her death in 1920. From 1923 a Miss Dobson took over, followed in 1931 by Miss West and in 1933 by Miss Mountain. Remembered Top School staff are Herbert William Reeve, who was the first head, and his daughter Ethel, an assistant. Mr Rogers became head in 1922, his staff at that time comprising Mr Sammonds, Miss Reay (who Mr Rogers married in 1942), Miss Lawton, Miss Reeve and Miss Beech. After the Infants joined the school in 1942, Miss Dean, Miss Doorbar and Miss Brookes joined the staff, to be followed at the end of the War by Mrs Warrender. Mr Tapley became Head in 1946. He took up another appointment in 1951, at which time Miss Turner became the new Headteacher.

Before 1870, School Logs were not compulsory. However, an annual report of the educational (and financial) health of Biddulph Moor School was expected, as this 1862 example shows.

THE NINTH ANNUAL REPORT

OF THE

BIDDULPH MOOR

Day and Sunday Schools

INSTITUTED 1852.

Committee of Management.

JAMES BATEMAN, ESQ., PRESIDENT
REV. W. H. HOLT   MR. R. MYOTT
MR. J. MYOTT   W. BRADBURY, Esq.
REV. FRANCIS GORDON, TREASURER and HON. SECRETARY

MASTER :—MR. HALL.

MISTRESS :—MRS. HALL.

REPORT.

THE Managers of the BIDDULPH MOOR DAY AND SUNDAY SCHOOLS, present their Ninth Annual Report with feelings of renewed gratitude to God for another year of favourable progress in the history of their Institution.

THE DAY SCHOOL

Register records the admissions and readmissions of 80 boys and 47 girls during the year ; making up a total of 91 boys and 58 girls on the books, with an average daily attendance of 90 scholars upon the whole number ; being an increase upon the last year of 11 daily, and 32 in total numbers.

BELOW:
Teacher Harry Caulton's wage slip
- see also page 13.

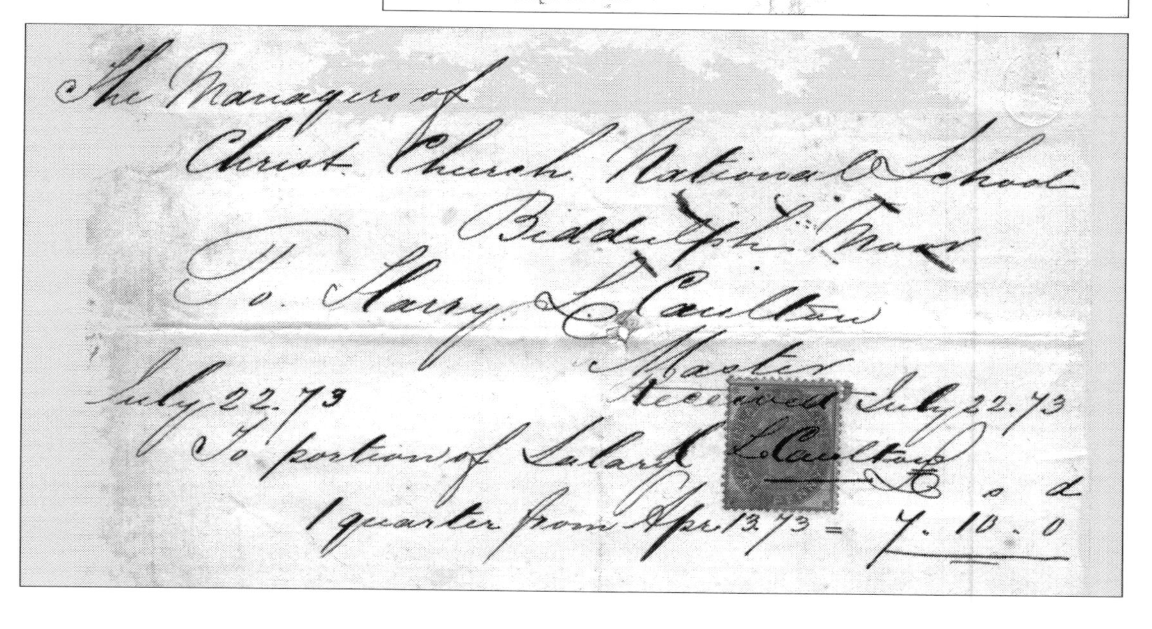

The Managers of
Christ Church National School
Biddulph Moor
To Harry L Caulton
Master
July 22.73
Received July 22.73
To portion of Salary
L Caulton
£ s d
1 quarter from Apr 13/73 = 7. 10. 0

She left in 1955, when Mr Smith Holmes took over the running of the school. In his retirement in 1971 he records his pleasure in teaching children *'whose sense of humour is second to none'* and his gratitude to *'a happy and hard-working staff'*. He makes a particular point of commending Ailsa Booth, his secretary for fourteen years and a former pupil at the school.

Ailsa

'When I went up to the Infants (1925) I didn't like it much and I stayed away a lot because my friends were older and they all went to Top School at the top of Church Lane. I stayed in the Infants' for two years, and what sticks in my mind is the old iron stove in the hall. Children would put their dinner near the stove to keep it warm, along with their wet clothes. Outside there were old slate toilets, and by School House some gardens where the boys from Top School grew vegetables and flowers. At seven I went up to Top School and I was really happy there. There were six classrooms and it was heated from a big coke oven. We used to sit on the heating pipes in the corridor to keep warm in winter. The playground was split in two by railings, boys in one part and girls in the other.

The Head was Mr Rogers. He was a lovely, cheerful man, strict but fair. He played the violin and the piano and set up a choir and an orchestra.

We sat at hinged desks, a boy and a girl to a desk. We wrote in ink in exercise books, and each day began with a prayer. Before you went in you lined up in the playground. When the whistle blew we had to get in line, then file in, girls through one door, boys the other, all making a clatter because of our clogs.

We had to know our tables forwards and backwards to twelves. The girls had cookery with Miss Jewel and darning and sewing with Miss Beech (later Mrs Brookes). One afternoon a week we walked down Nettlebeds track to Kingsfield in Biddulph for laundry practice. There were about fifteen girls. At the end of the afternoon we had to walk home. We learnt how to 'dolly' clothes and how to use a 'postle' which punched the clothes under the water. We also learned how to mangle, how to make starch and how to iron.

The girls did netball and rounders in PT, and at break we'd play hopscotch, top and whip and skipping. In English we had to recite poems by heart in front of the class.

One year I was Carnival Queen, and I was supposed to set an example to others. But I decided to sit on the bank below the school at lunch time, knowing the bank was out of bounds. Miss Beech found out and gave me lines to write. At least I wasn't caned. That would have really let the side down.'

Ewart Nixon started at the Infants in 1935, and a year later the bell tower was struck by lightning. I have no reason to conclude the two facts are in some way linked.

Ewart

'I stayed at the Infants for two years before going up the road to the Council School, or Top School as it was called then. The Infants was split into two classes in my time. Both classes were in the room overlooking Church Lane, and we went in the hall for a morning drink. I recall Miss Doorbar and Miss Mountain. In the Infants we concentrated on the 3Rs and wrote in exercise books with pencils and sometimes stick pens. It was cold in winter, and there was a big stove half way down the hall to provide some heat.

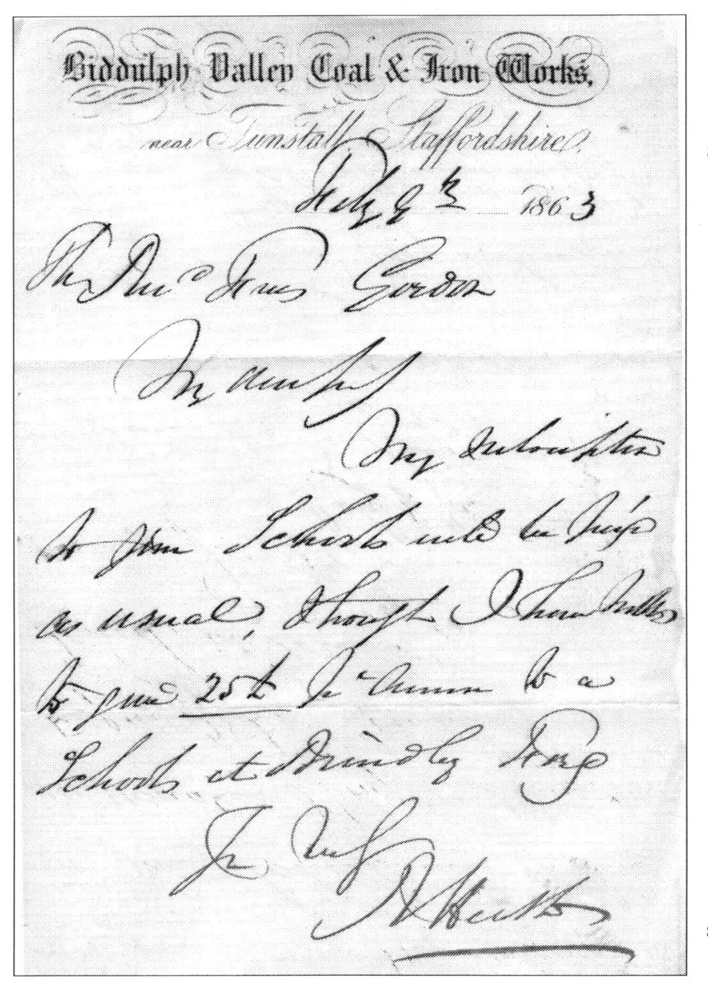
Biddulph Valley Coal & Iron Works,
near Tunstall Staffordshire.
July 9th 1863
The Revd James Gordon
My dear Sir
My subscription to your Schools will be [illegible] as usual, though I have settled to give 25£ per Annum to a Schools at Brindley Ford
Yours truly
R Heath

Local industrialist Robert Heath agrees to contribute to Biddulph Moor School in this 1863 letter - while pointing out he has already agreed to give £25 per annum to the school at Brindley Ford, near to his works and collieries.

By 1902 Biddulph Moor National School is referred to as an Infant School - although this is only a section of it. A modest requisition to last for 6 months.

Biddulph Moor Infant School. 28.9.0[illegible]

Probable cost of working materials for the ensuing 6 months

	£	s	d
Pictures for Object Lessons.	1	0	0
Stationery, Slates, Pencils Chalk &c.	1	2	6
Kindergarten Materials	1	2	6
Needlework Materials		6	0
Reading Sheets		10	0
	£4	1	0

Mr, H, L, Caulton

Sir

Take Notice

We the undersigned Trusts & Managers of Biddulph Moor Nat, School do hereby give you Notice that your term of Service as Master of the above School shall & will end on Midsummer Day next ensuing and that on and from that period you are and will be discharged from all the duties of Master of the said School and from all future interest in the same and the premises thereof by virtue of your office as Master — also at the same time discharged from the office of Organist and Choir master of Biddulph Moor Church — and that you are required at the expiration of this Notice to deliver over to one of the Managers of the said School the keys of the School & School House and all other and singular property with which you are entrusted by virtue of your office — Mrs Caulton is also by this Notice discharged from the duty of Sewing Mistress to the Girls of the above School at the same time —

Given & served this twenty fifth day of March in the year of our Lord One thousand eight hundred & seventy four

Francis Gordon
John Mellor
Robert Bateman
} Trusts & Managers

It seems that Harry Caulton, a master at Biddulph Moor School, blotted his copy book. But he wasn't to take his dismissal lightly, and took the Rev. Francis Gordon to court for wrongful dismissal.

Dongles
Wedy

My Dear Sir,

I am truly sorry to hear that you have been suffering from illness but heartily trust that ere this reaches you – all trace of it will have disappeared & that you will have been restored to yr usual sphere of usefulness.

As regards the additional length of front walls the estimate containing does appear unsuspicious, I think therefore it will be better to leave them (they will be the last things required) & allow the contract to stand at its present figure, & so proceed at once to work –

If you have any difficulty in procuring the old general ground plan you can readily supply the deficiency by furnishing an outline of the entire plot (excluding the interior cross fence & the footpath) & then get Lockett to place upon it in proprio situ the pile of buildings – thus –

A
Masters
A
Garden
A
Boys Playground
Girls Playground
Lane

The outline of this is from memory but it will shew the sort of thing required. Of course it must be on a much larger scale & the main sewer & other drains must be shewn, being marked in blue ink & their direction indicated by an arrow (→).

You must also on no account forget to explain that in the direction marked A.A A in the plan there is a deep valley so that the block of building cannot be moved further in that direction. Also the points of the compass

N
W E
S

must be there –

I shall be truly glad to hear that the works have been actually commenced & meanwhile am ever, my Dear Sir

very truly yrs

Jas. Bateman

School milk started when I moved to Top School. It was delivered by Mr Harvey of Wickenstone Farm and came in third of a pint bottles with straws. The Head of the school was Mr Rogers. He lived at the bottom of Woodhouse Lane in a big detached house. His wife died and he married one of the teachers, Miss Reay. He was very firm, as all the teachers were in those days, but he was fair too.

I remember one incident involving a lad who had been caned by Mr Rogers for doing something wrong. The lad went back to his seat in a temper, kicking the heating pipes as he went. Mr Rogers followed him, taking swipes at his bottom with the cane. The lad's father came up the next day and asked Mr Rogers if he had caned his son. When the Headmaster admitted he had and told him why, the lad's father replied: 'Cane him harder next time.'

The other teachers I remember are Miss Reay, Mrs Brookes, Miss Reeve, Miss Clark and Miss Dean. Mr Rogers also taught, and I learnt the tonic sol-fa from him. Another incident springs to mind. The prefects had to ring the bell for morning and afternoon school. On one occasion I took it into my head to shin up a drainpipe and ring the bell in the bell tower. Of course I was spotted, the reward being two strokes of the cane. I remember Mr Rogers' words quite clearly: 'I admire bravado in a lad, but you've set a bad example to the school.' I also remember being picked on by the school bully. One day I'd had enough and kicked him on the shin with my clogs. He never bullied me after that.

Apart from the 3Rs the boys did gardening. We had plots in a piece of ground behind the Infants School, where we cultivated a good range of vegetables. We were all proud of the results. I had very happy schooldays, but there were minor disappointments, such as when Mr Rogers told us we couldn't go to the promised woodwork classes at Knypersley because the woodwork teacher had been called up for the forces.

At playtimes the boys played football, cricket and marbles (or taws) on their side of the railings while the girls played skipping and hopscotch on theirs. I left in 1944, a year before the War ended.'

Jim Nixon first attended Top School in 1927, and some names from that time stay with him.

Jim

'For a time my reports were signed by Mrs Brookes. She was a stickler for discipline and taught at the school for a long time. She was in her nineties when she died. Ailsa Booth was in my class, and Annie May Gibson, who lived at Knawlow Farm.

The lavatories at Top School were not coupled to a sewer, and the night soil cart used to call. A neighbour used to grow prize-winning tomatoes, and the soil cart was the reason.

We were a ragged lot in tattered clothes and hand-me-downs. When it was cold we sat on the heating pipes to eat our dinner, and when there was a row the fighters settled their differences 'on top o' th' barn' - in other words, at Barn Farm on Hot Lane just above the school.

Apart from classroom lessons, we did Gardening and Woodwork, which I loved. The gardens were behind the Infants. We learnt how to make paths and plots and grew vegetables in the summer. Mr Rogers, the Head, or Mr Sammonds was in charge of ten to fifteen of us, while the girls did cooking.

LETTER OPPOSITE: James Bateman, who put up much of the money for Biddulph Moor School, liked to keep his finger on the pulse - even when holidaying in the Isle of Man. Letter to his builder probably 1851.

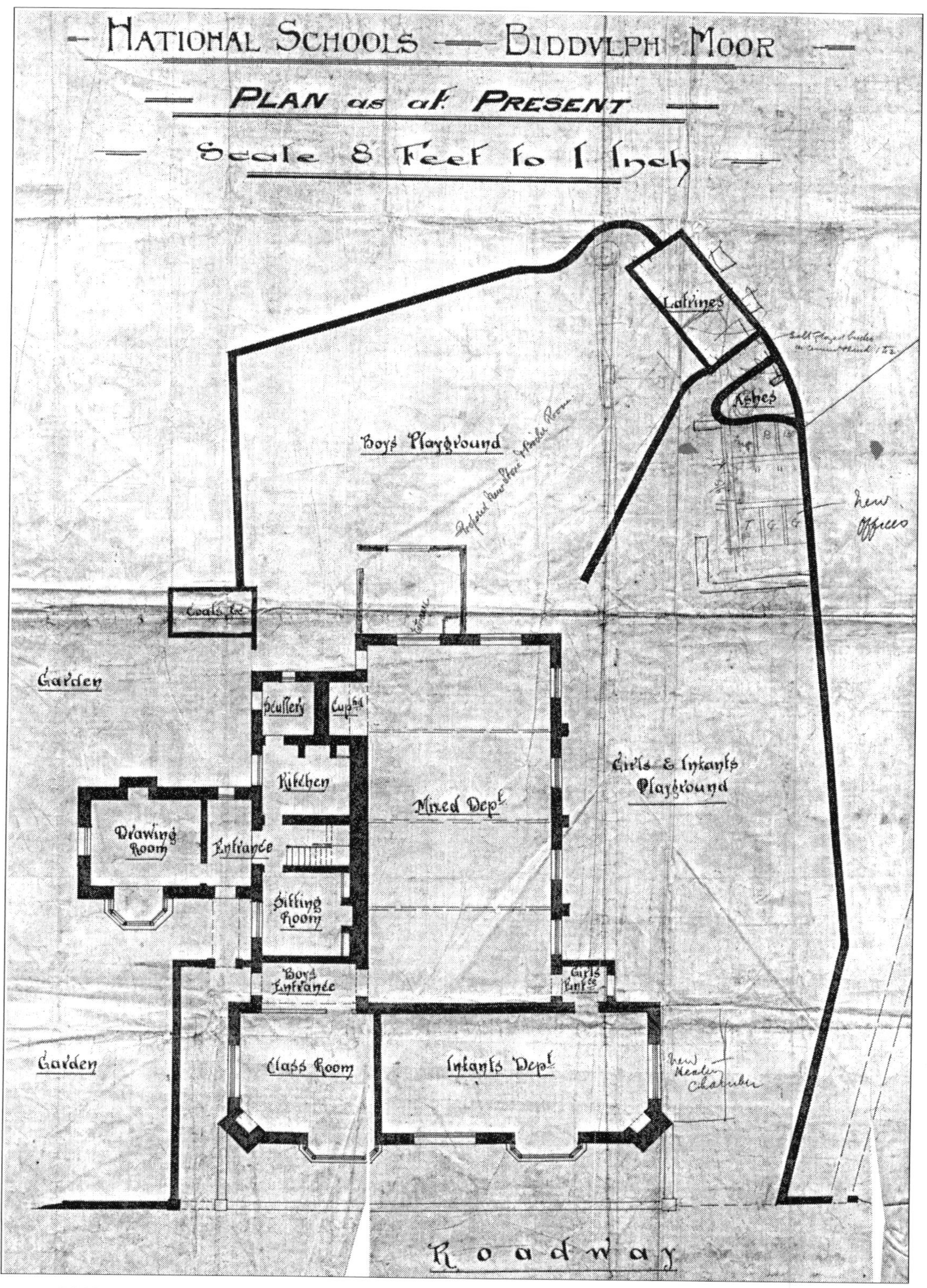

Biddulph Moor National School. Plan showing proposed new toilets and coal cellar, around 1890.

Biddulph Moor School, 1890s.

Top School class, 1921. Miss Reay left, Head Reeve, right.

A 1930's snap of Miss Reay (left) and Mrs Brookes.

Headmaster H W Reeve, 1900.

Top School and Infants staff, 1920. Head H.W. Reeve centre, Miss Reay extreme left, Mrs Brookes-to-be front row, left.

Mr Rogers was a good teacher, but I didn't care much for Mr Sammonds. He could be sarcastic and put you down.

We'd walk down to Knypersley to our Woodwork class on Friday afternoons. Our teacher was Herbert Law. He was a good teacher, but he had a short fuse and if the mood took him he'd hit you with a ruler or throw a piece of wood your way. I left in 1934, five years before the War started. I believe Mr Law was called up. I still have an oak coffee table I made at school when I was twelve.

The moment I left school, I began on the farm.'

Phyllis Nixon, who started at the Infants in 1931, remembers Christmases with particular pleasure:

Phyllis

'There was always a big Christmas tree in the first room (now the Parish Room) and I thought it was lovely because we couldn't afford one at home. They used to decorate it with baubles and tinsel ready for the Christmas Concert. The other thing that used to fascinate me was the beautiful staircase in School House (integral with the Infant School). There was nothing like it on the moor, where the houses had poky staircases.

I think Miss Reeve must have lived in School House at the time, because I remember her giving me and a friend a needlework basket to carry to Top School. On top of the basket were two little cakes - our reward for carrying the basket.'

Miss Reeve and Miss Lawton retired from Top School in 1942, the same year as Mr Rogers' marriage to Miss Reay. Agnes Pass recalls her time as a pupil there before the War:

Agnes

'Mr Rogers was the Head. The garden was next to School House where the boys tended their plots. When we went to school every spring, we'd collect different kinds of wild flowers for Miss Reay and put them in the hallways and in all the windows, little jars and bottles all named. Mr Rogers was very fond of her and they married. Unfortunately she was often unwell and had to go away a lot. She was a very highly strung person, but a very nice one.

Mrs Brookes was also at the school. If she took against you you were in trouble, but if she liked you you were all right. I was on her good side, thankfully, but some children could find themselves on her sharp side.'

In 1948, by the time Anne Newton started school, the Infants had moved to Top School. By then the 11+ had also been introduced. Anne was fortunate enough to secure a Grammar School place.

Anne

'The reason why I passed was our teacher, Mr Locker. He really crammed us for the exam, and I managed to get a place at Clayton Hall. To get there you had to catch a bus from Biddulph Moor to Biddulph, then another to Tunstall. At Tunstall I caught the school bus and that got me there in time. But if the weather was bad on the moor, the journey was well nigh impossible. Sometimes there were snow drifts and the bus home would only go as far as Knypersley, then you walked. I got home at seven o'clock one night with icicles on my hood, to be greeted with *'You're late!'*

Biddulph Moor School, early 1900s.

Biddulph Moor Infants' School, 1929.

Some memories of my time at school linger on. I remember the school air raid shelters off School Lane, the heap of coke for the heating and the one third pint milk bottles. But the sanitary conditions left much to be desired. The toilets stank, and I recall a fenced-off area near the school which I supposed was once part of the sewage disposal system in some way. I don't think the school was on mains sewers until about 1962.

The teachers I remember are Headmaster Mr Holmes, Mrs Warrender, Mrs Brookes and Mr Locker. Apart from the fact Mrs Brookes occasionally belted me, my time at Top School was a happy one, and when they found out I could play the cornet, I was in demand.'

Jane Doorbar first attended the Infants' in 1917, the year before the Great War ended.

Jane

School House was occupied by Mr Reeve, the Head of both schools. I remember he wore a goatee beard and pince-nez glasses and he sometimes had a dropper on the end of his nose as well. He used to have boys from Top School doing his garden for him.

The Infants' Mistress when I was there was Miss Dale, a lovely lady. I also remember Miss Pointon and Mrs Beech. There were two partitioned rooms facing the road and the hall was partitioned too. There was an open fire, but the cold would still seep into the place in winter. The yard was of blue brick, split into boys and girls sections like Top School. The boys could be unruly, but the stick was always to hand then.

Teacher Gertrude Doorbar (left) had no truck with naughty boys - she slapped their bare knees.

I went up to Top School in 1919. Mr Reeve was the Head until Mr Rogers took over. Mr Rogers had about six children, if I remember correctly, and three of them used to walk to Top School from Biddulph with him, where he had a rented house before the home he had built in Woodhouse Lane. His wife died later, and he married Miss Reay during the War. She was one of his teachers, a lovely woman.

Going back to the Twenties, when I was at Top School: in my time there the boys and girls were separated in the playground. The toilets were about fifty yards from the school and emptied by the night soil men and tipped on the fields. When the wind was in the wrong direction there was an awful stink. Likewise, the boiler ash was tipped on to the local lanes.

There were big radiators, but often it was really cold because the caretaker didn't get to school early enough to draw up the coke furnace. The teachers were strict, and I have memories of one of the women carrying a cane all the time, which she swished against her skirts as she walked.

We had cookery on Fridays and went down to Biddulph Central School for Laundry. In Cookery, we had a recipe and one egg divided between us all. Miss Jewel was the teacher. She came on a bike all the way from Congleton.

One thing I remember was going with the school to see the Prince of Wales at the Grange. He was in an open carriage. We were given a flag to wave, but weren't allowed into the grounds.'

Malcolm Locker, who taught at Top School from 1951-4, has pleasant memories of his time there:

Malcolm

'When I started teaching the leaving age was eleven, and we had to cram the children for the 11+ to compete with other schools. Quite a lot got through, but I always felt sad about those who had no envelope to take home to their parents to say they'd passed.

I worked mainly under Smith Holmes, who followed Miss Turner as Headteacher. He was a talented man, a good cricketer and pianist. Then there was Mrs Warrender - a delightful lady who took the reception class - Nelly Brookes and Mrs Camm. Mrs Camm was a local music teacher and pianist, and she was very good with the children.

A couple of incidents spring to mind. I recall we had a caretaker who didn't like coming to school in the dinner time to attend to the boiler, so she used to damp it down with the result the school could get very cold. One day the Head said to her: *'You've got to do something about the heating. It's freezing in the school.'*

She took exception to being told off and decided to get her own back by stoking up the boilers. The radiators started rattling and hissing and the place began to get red hot. I rang the heating engineer and he told us to get the kids out quick. So we marched them down the road to the Church Hall. After a while I said to Smith Holmes, *'I think I'll go back up and see what's going on.'*

So I pulled a towel around my mouth and went down into the furnace room. I found a shovel and dragged out the burning fuel. It took quite a while for the school to cool down.

Sometimes I had dealings with Billy Booth. I remember once a consignment of new desks arrived at the school and we couldn't decide what to do with the old ones. I started by taking them apart, putting the ironwork on one side for the rag and bone man and the wood on the other. I mentioned to Billy Booth, who I knew had a workshop, that I didn't know what to do with the wood. *'Leave it with me,'* came the answer. *'I'll plane it up. You have half for shelving and I'll have the other half for coffins.'* I found out later he had the contract to supply coffins for still-born infants.

They were great days, lovely kids and cooperative parents.'

Lillian Armitt was Senior Dining Room Assistant at Top School during Malcolm's time there. She retired in 1971, having witnessed many changes in the way the service was administered in Biddulph Moor.

Lillian

'There were no dinners at Top School before I started, just sandwiches for those who didn't go home. Then in 1952 they started to cook meals in Shepherd Street, Biddulph, and distributed them to schools in the area. The food arrived in insulated containers, potatoes in one, carrots in the other and so on. We had to ladle the food on to the children's plates, and kept the plates warm over the oven. We usually had ninety children to serve, and there was

Top School Top Class. Mr Tapley (Head) seated right. Back row centre, a fair-haired Mary Pointon. 1949.

Mrs Beech has an eclectic group for Christian Endeavour, 1952.

just two of us. It was hard work.

The containers were brought up by Whitehurst the butcher's, or they came by bus. When we'd cleared up and sterilized everything in boiling water we stacked them by the door to be returned when the next containers arrived.

I'd begin at eleven and finish at three. At eleven we set up the tables, and at twelve the children came in. Dinner break lasted an hour. After they went we had our dinner along with the staff. My wages were 1/11½d an hour.

After a while the system changed to self-service. Separate small containers were put on the tables on trays. There were six children to a table and one server who dealt out the food, so we were spared the job of dishing it out. These small containers arrived in a larger container in a van.

The ladies I worked with were Doris Warren, Lily Lancaster, Mary Pointon and Nita Nichols. Among the staff I recall Mrs Warrender, a lovely woman who took the Infants and Mrs Myatt. Mrs Brookes was very strict. I knew of one little girl who used to cry every morning because she was afraid of Mrs Brookes. I also remember Mr Locker and Mr Cooper, who were both very nice. And among the children I remember are Douglas Bailey and Alan Davies. They'd always have a great plateful and come back for seconds.

But one name that particularly springs to mind is Miss Drewery. She was the meals supervisor, and she laid down the law in no uncertain terms, checking cupboards, plates, everything. Worse still, she'd come at any time without letting us know, sometimes several times a month. Luckily she took to me, and was very nice to me when I retired.

I really loved my time at the school. There were no bosses to speak of. Everyone pulled together.

We leave a final comment to a Schools' Inspector, who was quick to notice the number of children who shared the same surname at Top School:

'The admission registers give evidence of family relationships among many of the children. For example, 22 of the 41 children entered under 'W' have the same surname, and the only surname under 'M' occurs 13 times.'

Top School Log, July 10th 1935.

Biddulph Moor Council (or Top) School, now Moor First, 1930s.

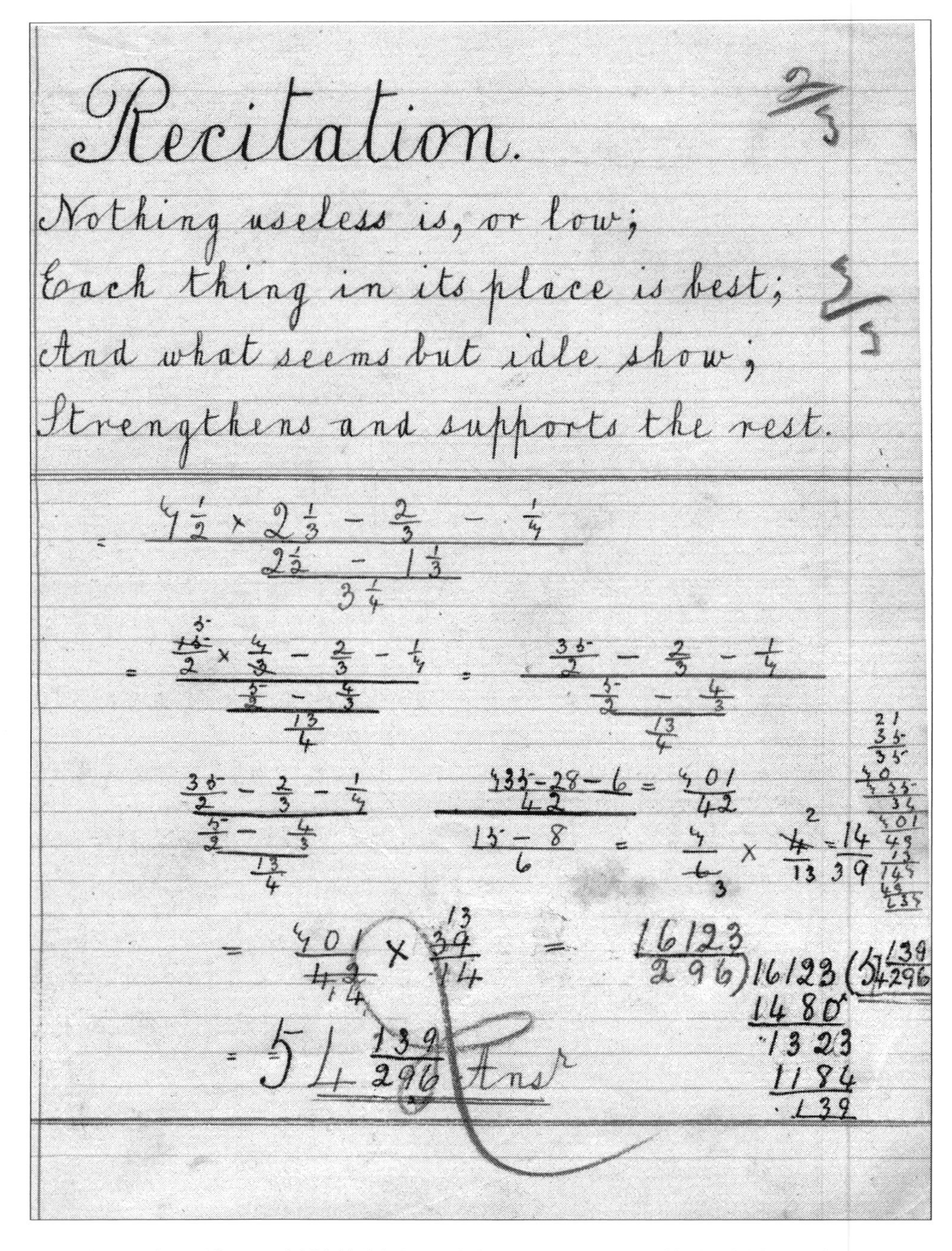

Recitation.

Nothing useless is, or low;
Each thing in its place is best;
And what seems but idle show;
Strengthens and supports the rest.

$$= \frac{4\frac{1}{2} \times 2\frac{1}{3} - \frac{2}{3} - \frac{1}{4}}{\frac{2\frac{1}{2} - 1\frac{1}{3}}{3\frac{1}{4}}}$$

$$= \frac{\frac{35}{2} - \frac{2}{3} - \frac{1}{4}}{\frac{\frac{5}{2} - \frac{4}{3}}{\frac{13}{4}}} = \frac{\frac{210-8-3}{12}}{\frac{15-8}{6}}$$

$$\frac{433-28-6}{42} = \frac{401}{42} \qquad \frac{15-8}{6} = \frac{4}{6} \times \frac{4}{13} = \frac{14}{39}$$

$$= \frac{401}{42} \times \frac{39}{14} = \frac{16123}{296}$$

$$= 54\frac{139}{296} \text{ Ans}^r$$

A page from 12 year old Biddulph Moor School pupil Emma Bailey's 1905 copy book.

COPY FOR THE INFORMATION OF THE MANAGERS AND FOR ENTRY IN THE LOG BOOK (ART. 23)

W B & L (x)—44804—200

Form 35.

Letters should be addressed—
"The Secretary,
Board of Education,
Whitehall,
London, S.W.,"
and should show the complete postal address and designation of the writer.

BOARD OF EDUCATION,

WHITEHALL, LONDON, S.W.,

24 MAY 1906

Please write at the head of any reply—

STAFFS. *Local Education Authority.*

BIDDULPH MOOR NATIONAL *School.* *No.* 33.

SIR,

I am directed to forward a copy of a Report made by H.M. Inspector upon the above School.

I am to call attention to the Annual Report for 1904 and to the Official letters of 28th April 1905, 30th May 1905 and 13th March 1906, and to state that unless satisfactory proposals for the improvement of the premises and relief of the continued overcrowding at the above-named School are submitted to the Board of Education through the Local Education before 31st July 1906 together with a definite assurance that the necessary alterations will be executed without undue delay, the Board will be unable to recognize the premises as providing Public Elementary School accommodation after 31st May 1907.

I am, therefore, to request that the Board may be informed at an early date what steps it is proposed to take in the matter.

Article 23 of the Code requires that any report of an Inspector, and any remarks made thereon by the Board for communication to the Managers of the School, must as soon as received be entered *in extenso* in the Log Book and signed by the Correspondent.

I am, SIR,

Yours faithfully,

H. M. Lindsell

By 1906, overcrowding at Biddulph Moor School was getting so desperate the Board of Education was threatening to withhold funding. Fortunately, money was forthcoming and Top School was built two years later.

BIDDULPH MOOR COUNCIL SCHOOL

BULB SHOW and CONCERT

Wednesday February 11th, 1925.

PROGRAMME

6 p.m. Bulb Show open, in Bulb Room.

6-30. In Church Room. STANDARD I. present

"SNOW WHITE and ROSE RED"

In Two Scenes

Snow White—Mona Battersby.
Mother—Vivian Foden.
Bear—William Proctor.
Red Rose—Muriel Hulme.
Dwarf—Arnold Moores.
Eagle—John Shufflebotham.

Fairies and Dancers. Trained by Miss Beech.

6-50. STANDARD IV. present

"COME LADS AND LASSIES"

Fairy Queen—Fanny Battersby. **Puck**—George H. Goodwin.
Nick—Ernest Warren.

Country Girls—
Frances Lovatt. Connie Biddulph.
E. A. Biddulph. Agnes Beech.

Country Boys—
Donald Gallimore. Ernest Nixon.
William Stonier.

Trained by Miss Reay.

7-15. STANDARD VI. present

"THE MAGIC FAN"

A Fairy Play in Three Scenes.

Scenes 1 and 3—Queen Ruella's Palace. Scene 2—King Pippin's Palace.

Princess Crystal—Florrie Battersby **Queen Ruella**—Hilda Bailey.
King Pippin—John Bailey.
Queen Pippin—Elsie Holland.
Prince Garnet—(their Son)—Lily Lancaster.
Golconda—Edwin Rogers. **Baron Blunderbuss**—Dennis Bradbury.
Count Lakadai—Jack Fletcher. **Griselda**—(Governess)—Olive Beech.
The Red Magician—Jane Brough.
Fairy Pearl—Jane Lovatt. **Jester**—Walter Brown.

Pages, Pippin's Soldiers, and Fairies in Chorus.

Princess of Persia, Polly Bradbury

ORCHESTRA. Violins—Miss Beech. Mr. A. Bailey.
'Cellos—Messrs Shufflebotham and Sutton. **Pianist**—Mrs. Booth.

F. Rowley, Printer, Biddulph.

Top School concert programme, 1926. Some familiar names.

1927 Top School Football Team. Headmaster Mr Rogers left.
Eric Haywood, holding the ball, later played for Blackpool.

Top School Football Team, 1937. Front row from left: F Bailey, T Wilshaw, E Biddulph, F Machin, W Brown.
Back row from left: H Nixon, J Beech, J Harvey, A Barlow, R Shufflebotham, J Randell

Top School in musical form, 1940s. Headmaster Mr Rogers on right.

Chapter 2
Farms, Mines and Mills

'We were all given six hens and we had to look after them. When we had a broody hen we were shown how to make a nest of a clod with straw on top. We had our own dish to put our eggs in, and Mr Bradbury from Biddulph would come every Thursday to collect them. That gave us our pocket money.'

from *My Childhood Memories on the Moor* by Annie Ethel Cook, describing her life at Firwood House Farm in the early Twenties.

Apart from shop-keeping - which is the subject of a later chapter - mining, quarrying, farming and the two local mills were the mainstay of the pre-war village economy. Miners left for their shift at Chatterley Whitfield, the Victoria Colliery or Norton Pit, and the miners' buses to and from the moor were always full. By 1937 velvet cutting at the fustian had come to an end, the post-war building given over first to paint-making, then to joinery. The shirt mill survived until the '50s and was later demolished, and of the 20 + shops which made a living before the war, only three survive. Farming continues despite Government red tape and supermarket sourcing, but the old 'wheelbarrow' farms of an acre or so are largely a thing of the past. Newcomers to the village typically commute to work, the only substantial employer at the time of writing being Mitras Composites, producing glass-reinforced composite products for utilities, aerospace and transport.

Bailey's Shirt Factory, founded by local businessman and choirmaster Aaron Bailey around 1922, was created from the outer-buildings of a smallholding he owned. Initially it was a modest concern, consisting of a few machines powered by a diesel engine which also generated current for lighting. Shirts were produced from cotton, wool and mixed fibres. Although machines did the cutting, button-stitching and pressing was done by hand. On completion the shirts were packed in cane skips and taken to Congleton Station en route to a Manchester warehouse. The factory went from strength to strength, becoming known as Bailey's Manufacturing Company. Shortly before the War it was taken over by Ben Iredale, a Wilmslow businessman who married Eva Shufflebotham, a local girl. Elsie Evans began working there in 1938.

Elsie

'I was fourteen when I started at the mill, working for Ben Iredale. He used to travel to Biddulph Moor every day from Wilmslow in a big car. By that time the factory had grown and about fifty of us worked there. I was a sewer, making pyjamas and shirts. Later I did a lot of homeworking, sewing cuffs on to sleeves with our hand-sewing machine. That could be tricky.

The pay was 7/6d for a dozen sleeves, which arrived in packs. My sister used to bring them from the factory and take them back with her when I'd done. When I got used to it I could do five dozen a week. If the stitching and button-holing wasn't just so you'd get told off.

Ben Iredale travelled all over to get orders. He decided on the cloth and patterns, so we made plain and fancy pyjamas and shirts, a variety. Apart from a man who serviced the

Mary Pass - mother of MP Joan Walley - at the Shirt Factory in 1935.

Jane Bailey, Ailsa Booth nee Turner and Mary Pass in the Shirt Factory yard, 1935.

Lunch break at the Shirt Factory. Alan Turner with ladies Beardmore, Wilshaw, Smith and Pass, around 1935.

Working the land, two views of Rock End c. 1930.

machines, the workforce was nearly all women. Jobs came word of mouth.

When the War came we switched to khaki shirts, and we had a job to keep up with the orders. When the War ended, we switched to demob shirts. We clocked on from 8am to 5.30pm, and you could stay over for extra pay.

When Mr Iredale wasn't about, Eadie (Edith) Holland was in charge as manageress. She would start the machines at eight, just before we arrived. Once or twice there were rats after scraps. I remember she once picked up a spade and killed one.

There was a big stove at the bottom end of the mill, and if the wind wasn't right it would smoke us out. It could be so cold in winter we had to work with our coats on. There was a floor for cutting, one for inspecting and a room for pressing shirts and packing them into boxes, six to a box. The irons were big steam irons you pulled down, or flat irons. Shirts had to be folded in a certain way and pinned.

We had an hour off for dinner. The only other break would be a visit to the toilets, just old wooden seats over a tub. Eadie always had a big bunch of keys and she locked up at the end of the day.

By the early '50s orders began to dry up. Ben Iredale would go on the balcony and give us a speech, usually to tell us we were on short time. Eventually the mill closed down and was later demolished. Three bungalows were built on the site. We were like a big, happy family, really.'

The fustian had a more chequered career than the shirt factory. Up until 1937 it had provided work for many of the locals. Ewart Nixon believes the last batch of velvet made there was for Buckingham Palace. Both Jane and he recall that the firm was then owned by Jackson's of Congleton.

Fustian cutters Florrie Biddulph, Beatty Biddulph and Lizzie Nixon pose in their overalls and clogs, 1929/30.

Girls from the Shirt Factory enjoying themselves in this late 40s shot.
Edith Holland (overseer) back row, left. Marian Flynn extreme right.

Edith and Marian enjoy a Post-War lunch break at the Shirt Factory.

The cutting room at the Shirt Factory. Jenny Gibson nearest camera, Marian looking on. 1950s.

Velvet making at the fustian, 1924.
Annie Biddulph, Polly Bould, Connie Biddulph and Lizzie Nixon are among those posing for the camera.

Miners, probably at Whitfield or the Bull, probably late 1920s.

Jane

'Jackson's also had a fustian mill at Fegg Hayes. At first material was brought up to Biddulph Moor by horse and cart in massive rolls, and later by motor lorry. It was cut with knives - a very skilled job in those days - and shipped back to Congleton for dyeing. Clogs were worn by the cutters. They had to walk so far when they were cutting, clogs were the only footwear that could stand the wear and tear.'

Velvet manufacture had already ceased by the outbreak of the Second World War, by which time the factory was being used as a billet for British, then US troops. At the end of the war it reverted to limited industrial use, first as a paint factory, then as a joinery, and by the early '60s, producing plastics. By 1970 truck-maker ERF was producing fibreglass components for the haulage industry, having demolished part of the old fustian and in 1981 erected a purpose-built factory on the site. The remaining part of the fustian buildings are now used by Mitras Composites, who are again engaged in the production of glass-reinforced products.

Ken Pointon, who worked for the Biddulph Urban District Council, remembers the situation after the War.

Ken

First to come was Parr's from Tunstall, who made paint. They stayed until the early '50s. They had a problem, though. The only sewer was 4" pipe dug down to Biddulph during the war. It wasn't wide enough for whatever they were putting down it, and the paint used to block the drain. Around 1958 a proper sewer was put in by the council, Donald Machin being the contractor. Following Parr's came Horton and Sons, who ran a joinery business.

Mary, Ken's wife, takes up the thread.

Mary

'Mr Horton used to live at the Knypersley end of the mill. He had a nice place, and he even planted roses in front of the mill. Mr brother used to drive a wagon for him, and I worked there for a time in the '50s. They made furniture - tables, chests, shelving, all sorts of things. They seemed to do all right, and quite a few from the village worked there. My job was to knock the nails fully in using a punch, then fill the holes. Mr Horton went on until at least 1957, when he retired. Then the Edwards Brothers took over. They made plastics.'

While the mills provided for women, many of the men found work in the local mines. Some made the journey to the pit on foot; most caught the miners' buses which began picking up at the Rose and Crown. The local mining community was able to meet at the Miners' Welfare, a capacious building erected at the end of Gun Battery Lane in 1935 to replace the wooden Workingmen's Club which had until then stood on land adjacent to the Co-op building. The Miners' Welfare boasted an expansive bowling green and other amenities intended to serve the needs of those employed in nearby collieries.

Jane

'Miners' buses began to run about 1922, when the roads were made up. There were three buses to coincide with shifts: 5am, 1pm and 9pm. They were always blue with smoke. I remember one bus was owned by Elijah Bailey at the top of Leek Lane. One day the message got through all was not well, and one of the miners went to tell the others waiting outside the Rose and Crown: *'Come on, lads, we'll have to walk to the pit. The bus has just caught fire!' The bus never ran again.'*

Ewart and Ken both remember the blue fug shrouding the home-coming miners' buses.

Ken

'The last bus up was so full of smoke you couldn't see inside. They were all smoking, some smoking twist. Sometimes there were 90 men on a single decker, and if they picked up a farmer with a bag of coal they'd put it on the mudguard. The drivers got used to you. They'd deliver a prescription or wait for you by the stop if you were expected but hadn't arrived. After the War, the drivers were Arthur Ball and Frank Moss, and the conductors were Charlie Lancaster and George Kempster.'

Hezekiah Beech with trowel, around 1935.

Mary's father was a 'rope man' in charge of a team maintaining the coal tub cables. He retired in 1955 after 52 years in the colliery. Anne's father, a keen amateur boxer and a committed bandsman, worked at Whitfield Colliery, the sound of his homecoming clogs a signal to his wife to get the tin bath out. Jane's father was a collier before the coming of the miners' buses, and made the daily journey from the top of Hot Lane to Black Bull Colliery on foot, ready for an eight hour stint on the face. Despite the demands of the job, they still found time to tend their plots and to take an active part in village life. Jane recalls that farming in the '20s could be equally gruelling.

Jane

'We had to borrow a pony from Harvey's at haymaking. We tedded the hay by hand with rakes and if it rained it had to be done over again. When we weren't hay-making me and my sisters were churning butter using a dash churn. That was really hard work. Then we had to deliver milk. One winter the roads were blocked. I set out to deliver and my wire-haired terrier wanted to come too. He kept getting stuck in the snow at Robin Hill, his legs were so short. Still, the hard work didn't do us much harm. My dad was still cutting four acres with a scythe until he was seventy-four.'

Jim Nixon's father bought 28 acre Bradda (Braddow) Farm in 1915. By the time Jim left school in 1934, there wasn't much about farming he didn't know.

Jim

'Before the war we had 18 shorthorns. You were up first thing in the morning, hand milking, then the Co-op came around to collect it about 8.30am. My mother made butter and cheese

Hay bailing at Bradda Farm, 1948.

Jim's 'little grey Ferguson', 1948

BELOW:
Jim in Sunday Best, 1932.

BELOW:
Anne Newton's mother scything at David's Bank. 1930s.

for sale, and in the war we made butter for our own use by shaking cream up in a toffee jar. It took about twenty-five minutes.

My mother used to go on the bus to Tunstall with baskets of eggs and butter. The big houses near the park would give her good seconds' clothes for us to wear in exchange. I used to go to Leek Market with my father, too. He had an Austin 12, and we'd put a crate of eggs in the back packed in straw, and sometimes a hen crate to sell at market.

In the farm each cow had its own stall, with its name and a date. The dates referred to when the cow was served by a bull. Before mains water they had to be turned out twice a day to drink from the pond, and if the weather was bad we brought water up in buckets. When mains water and power came in the '30s things were much easier. The cows just pressed a button with their nose when they wanted water. We also kept two or three breeding sows. They could be nasty when they were farrowing, so we had a farrowing crate to keep the piglets and sow separate. When the piglets were six weeks old I had to cut off their testicles so they wouldn't serve their sisters. You held the piglet between your legs while another man cut off its testicles with a razor blade and applied black oil, an antiseptic. Occasionally a piglet was born which was neither male nor female, and we had a name for it - a Will-Jill.

You were forever mucking out, feeding livestock and hens. Summer haymaking was done by hand using a horse-drawn mowing machine which cut a yard at a time. That job needed five days of settled weather.

We had a horse named Doll. She was one of the family, and when you fetched her from the field she'd let you get up on her back without a saddle and take you home. She was as gentle as an old shoe. After Doll we had Captain, a gelding, a good, strong horse. One night he got loose and ate some potatoes which gave him colic. I didn't know then that if a horse had colic you had to walk it round and round and never let it lie down or there'd be a twist in the bowels and that was it. So old Captain succumbed, unfortunately.

A horse was more a friend. He knew what you were thinking. When we had to plough during the War we had two horses working together. We used to borrow Old Jack and he had a spring halt, which meant he walked cocking one leg high as if he were lame. One horse would walk in the furrow and at the end 'Whoa, turn back' and he'd do it. They are very sensible animals, but when they're young they can be big-headed. We called it 'collar-proud', full of beans.

We sometimes brought in a local pig killer. The blood was caught in a bucket for black puddings. We sold the pigs to Brown's of Hanley and we used to tell them we had so many porkers and bacon to send in. Hay went in the barns for winter feed. It had to be totally dry or it would lose its nature and give the cows husk. There was a saying: 'It doesn't cost much to make good hay, but it costs a lot to make bad hay'. That was as true then as now.

The man who showed me how to castrate piglets also showed me how to put a ring through a bull's nose. You had to get it with its head over the stall door, with the ring ready and a red hot poker. You held the bull with pincers and did the job very quickly. It wouldn't be allowed now.

There were all sorts of medicines for the cattle. A Congleton man named Stubbs used to call on his bike and trailer. One favourite was Cheshire Bottle, used if cows were a bit shivery. It was a warming mixture, like Indian Brandy. It didn't do any harm either, because my dad used to have a swig now and again. The horses had to be shod for summer work along flinty lanes, and we took them to Phil Taylor at Knypersley, then later to Charlie Perkins near Endon Well.

Before mains water and electricity we had to rely on a ten-foot well. Lighting was either by candle or oil lamp. Things didn't really change too much until after the War, when we had our first tractor, a little grey Ferguson. Later on, I decided to try my hand at mink farming, which was quite successful for a time.

I still do a bit of farming. They say you keep going to keep going. But those early days, when I had itchy feet and wanted to make something of myself - those times stay with me.'

Jane Doorbar helps Sam Harvey make hay in this late 20s picture.

It doesn't get any easier. Jane Doorbar, sister Mary and Jane's sister in law manage to bury the hay wagon. Early 30s.

Farmer or not, no one living on Biddulph Moor could be wholly removed from the land.

Ewart

'When I was a lad me and a friend used to drive a local farmer's cows to Nettlebeds Farm where Dennis Bailey, father of Bill and Howard, kept a bull. The farmer would pay Dennis half-a-crown to have the cow serviced - and I learnt about life in the process.'

A rural area will inevitably produce its fair share of (apocryphal?) farming stories. Ewart ends with one of them.

Ewart

'A pig was pushed in a barrow to a neighbouring farm to be serviced by the boar. When the boar had finished, the pig was returned to the farm. The next day the farmer looked high and low for the pig. Eventually he found it - in the barrow waiting for a return trip!'

Biddulph Moor Male Voice Choir, taken at Top School late 40s. Seated, from left: Wm Brookes (President), Frank Tatton (Conductor), Elizabeth Booth (Accompanist)

Village outing, 1930s - possibly a Sunday School trip.

Chapter 3
High Notes

Hospital Saturday was a carnival, really. It was always led by the Biddulph Moor Brass Band and the dignitaries used to ride in horse-drawn coaches. There was the Queen and attendants, and the maypole dancers were trained by Mrs Stanway. When I was sixteen Mary Lovatt, Annie Lovatt, Jane Lovatt and myself entered our farm wagon as 'Seaside Scenes'. I still have the photographs.

from *My Childhood Memories on the Moor* by Annie Ethel Cook, in the 1920s.

The children wore patriotic costumes, and, bearing flags, marched to Mr Gibson's field where a thanksgiving service was held by the Rev. Fletcher. The children entertained the assembly with dancing and a football match. Biddulph Moor Band was in attendance afterwards. Tea was later served to all scholars and each child was given a Jubilee Mug by Biddulph Urban District Council, who were responsible for the financial arrangements.

Top School Log, describing events around King George V's Silver jubilee in 1935.

Before the age of mass motoring and television, few other villages could have rivalled Biddulph Moor in its ability to amuse itself. That this small community could have produced a prize-winning brass band is in itself remarkable, but its range of activities also extended to choirs, concerts, a jazz band, a successful football team and the locally famous Hospital Saturday. Almost everyone was involved in some capacity, and both church, chapel and school played an active role throughout the year.

Beacon Building on Bailey's Hill to celebrate coronation of George V1, 1937

Hospital Saturday records exist from at least 1908 to 1961, and although no war-time accounts have come to light, it was proposed in March, 1939, by Mr Machin the then Secretary, that Hospital Saturday *'carries on as usual'*.

The event evolved from a need to provide funds for health care, and money raised was distributed to local hospitals with donations continuing long after the introduction of the post-war National Health Service. Ewart Nixon has abiding memories of this seminal day in the village calendar.

Ewart

'A local girl was made Rose Queen, but there were others who worked at the fustian

Baby Show, 1946, at Top School. Proceeds to Greenway Moor Band.

Baby Show prizewinners, 1946.

because I also recall a Velvet Queen and a Cotton Queen. The carnival was held at Knawlow farm, and all the wagons were decked out in flowers made by the local women. Most of the attractions were provided by the locals, but one or two were brought in from elsewhere. I remember the Great Galvani put in an appearance at one time. His speciality was to pull a coal wagon with his teeth, and as an encore he'd attach a rope to his neck and swing around a pole until his feet were off the ground. Maypole dancing was popular too, but the Greasy Pole and Greasy Pig events were a big draw. Someone would try to shin up a greased pole to retrieve a £5 note pinned to the top. When that failed he'd try his hand at wrestling a greased pig. It inevitably escaped into the crowd. The Greenway Moor Prize Band always turned out a memorable performance. They were famous in the area and many locals could boast at least one member of their family was involved. All in all it was a very joyous occasion.'

Joke policeman Joseph Turner marshals the crowds at Knawlow Farm. 1930s.

Anne Newton's musical legacy began with her grandfather Ben Fletcher. She remembers her family's commitment to the Greenway Moor Prize Band was all consuming.

Anne

'My father's family already had musical experience when they came to Biddulph Moor around 1911. They arrived pushing a handcart, with their possessions, all the way from Burbage in Derbyshire, where they had lived until then. There was my grandfather Ben and his children Alice, Frank, and my father Jack. Harry and Tommy were born later, on the moor. Graham was the youngest.

Apart from Alice, they all played an instrument. Dad played the trombone. Ben, Frank and Graham played the cornet, Harry the horn and Tommy the euphonium. Aunt Alice was in demand as a soprano.

They settled at Ridgefields in two rented cottages. All the men worked in the local mines except for Tommy, who went into the building trade before and after his service in the War. Dad and his brothers married local girls and joined the Biddulph Moor Band. They were all obsessed with band music. Once my father tripped over the cat and bent his trombone. He had a short fuse at the best of times, and if he'd had the chance he would have throttled the cat.

Soon the next generation was playing too. Alice's son Ian played tenor horn and baritone for Greenway and Doulton's, and Tommy's son Barry played Tenor horn in the Greenway band. Dad formed a junior band and they'd practise at home. Sometimes my mother would go out and leave them to it, although she must have been used to it because her brother Arthur played the B-flat Bass. Later, they practised at the Methodist Sunday School. Dad also

Hospital Saturday, 1930. Interested bystanders include Frank Hulme, second from left.

Dance troupe enjoys the sun off Leek Lane, 1946.

BIDDULPH MOOR HOSPITAL SATURDAY, 1926.

Balance Sheet

Receipts.	£	s	d	Expenditure.	£	s	d
Balance from 1925.	£5	2	8	From Emergency Fund £		12	0
do (Emergency Fund)	5	0	0	North Staffs Infirmary	25	4	0
House to house Collection.				Macclesfield G Hospital	2	2	0
Children's Boxes	4	6	6	Llanfairfechan Home	2	10	0
Messrs Hall's Workmen	1	2	0	Cripples' Aid Society	2	2	0
Mr Arrowsmith		10	6	Congleton M. Hospital	5	5	0
New Inn		5	6	Devonshire Hosp (Buxton)	4	4	0
Subscriptions, [See list]	7	17	4				
Rose and Crown Box	2	11	6				
B.M & Dt Homing Society		16	6	Balance in hand		12	0
Church Collections, including Oddfellows Parade	6	0	0				
Wesleyan Ch. do.		8	6				
Collection, Band Concert	1	7	9				
Watch Competition	7	2	3				
Total £42 ,, 11 ,, 0				Total £42 ,, 11 ,, 0			

Presented, and passed at a Meeting of the Committee held January 19th, 1927.

H. W. Reeve Hon. Sec,
C. R. Hall Hon. Treasurer.

List of Donations

Mr. C. R. Hall	£ 2 ,, 2 ,, 0	Mr. H. W. Reeve	£ 1 ,, 0 ,, 0
,, Arrowsmith	10 ,, 6	Dr Murphy	10 ,, 6
,, W. Nixon	10 ,, 0	Miss Reeve	10 ,, 0
Miss Lawton	10 ,, 0	Mrs. C. R Hall	10 ,, 0
Mr T. Greenlagh	5 ,, 0	Mr G. Lawton	5 ,, 0
Mrs. M. Gregory	5 ,, 0	Mr. T. Shufflebotham	5 ,, 0
Mr J. Stanway	5 ,, 0	,, J. Lancaster	4 ,, 4
,, Hammersley	2 ,, 6	,, P. Stanway	2 ,, 6

Total £7/17/4

The 1926 Hospital Saturday accounts show a healthy balance.

The original handwritten accounts for 1926 Hospital Saturday

		£	s	d
	Balance from 1924-5.	5	2	8
	do Emergency Fund	5	0	0
House & House Collection	Rev. Iron		5	6
	By Children's Boxes	4	6	6
	Mr. Arrowsmith		10	6
	" Workmen of Messrs C. R. Hall & Co	1	2	0
Subscriptions	Mr. C. R. Hall	2	2	0
	" Arrowsmith		10	6
	" F. W. Reeve	1	0	0
	" Wm Hixon		10	0
	Mr. [illegible]		10	6
	Mrs Gregory (Widow)		5	0
	Mr. Hammersley		2	6
	Miss Reeve		10	0
	Rose & Crown	2	11	6
Nov 7th	Church Parade of Oddfellows £3/8/- " Collection £2/12/-	6	0	0
" 17th	B. Moor & District Friendly Society		16	6
Subscription	Mr. E. Lawton		5	0
	" T. Greenough		5	0
	" T. Shufflebotham		5	0
	" T. Stoneway (R. Hill)		2	6
	Wesleyan Collection		8	6
	Mr. Stoneway (R. Hill)		5	0
	Mr. C. R. Hall		10	0
Jan 1927.	Band Collection at Concert	1	7	9
	Whistle Competition	6	15	6
Children's Boxes	Jane Lovatt & Polly Bradbury 11 " 7; Annie Lovatt & Agnes Moores 1 " 3 " 10½; Janet Moores, Mary [illegible] & Connie [illegible] 16 " 3; Annie Bailey & Doris Bailey 8 " 4; Fanny Butterley & Agnes Beech 6 " 6; [illegible] & [illegible] Lancaster 7 " 6½; Phyllis Machin & Phyllis Smith 12 " 5 — £4 " 6 " 6	Miss Smith	10	0
		Per F. W. Fletcher (W.C.)	6	9
		Mr. Lancaster	4	4
		£42	11	0

		£	s	d
	Emergency Fund (T. Butterley)		12	0
Oct 6th	To N. Staffs. Infirmary	21	0	0
Dec 10th	Macclesfield Gen. Hosp.	2	2	0
do	Llanfairfechan Home	2	10	0
Dec 11th	Cripples' Home	2	2	0
" 16th	Congleton Memorial Hospital	5	5	0
Jan 1927 24th	North Staffs. Infirmary	4	4	0
do	Devonshire Hospital (Buxton)	4	4	0
	Balance in Hand		12	0
		£42	11	0

Velvet Queen Connie Biddulph (left) attended by maids Beattie Biddulph, Jane Biddulph, Rene Stanway and Phyllis Armitt, 1935.

The Shirt Mill float. Biddulph Moor Carnival, around 1935.

Ailsa Turner, Queen, takes leave of Doris Hackett, retiring Queen, in Hospital Saturday Carnival, 1932.

Biddulph Moor Jazz band, early 1920s. Ailsa's father Joseph Turner conducts, while hatted and hirsute Billy Skelton, later a well-known bandsman, with trombone to left.

Maypole dancing at Knawlow Farm. Hospital Saturday, 1920s

Hospital Saturday 1931. Doris Hackett sporting the crown.

Biddulph Moor girls Evelyn Stanway, Annie Hassall, Ailsa Turner and Jenny Bailey appear in the 1929 carnival, held at Hayden's Fields.

Cotton Queen - but only for a year. Gladys Stanway reigns, with Ailsa, Mary Pass, Dorothy Stanway, Clarice Biddulph in attendance. Jack Gallimore and Harold Brown seemingly unimpressed.

Hospital Carnival Committee, probably mid 20s. Sitting, from left: Messrs Stanway, Machin, Reeve, Hall, Beech. Standing, from left: Messrs A and S Bailey, Knight, Wilshaw, Lawton, Chaddock, Machin, Turner, Gregory, Elkin, Lancaster, Sammonds.

A pleasant day for this 1932 carnival.
Ailsa Turner nee Booth occupies the Queen's throne as retiring Queen Doris Hackett looks on.

Christ Church Queen and attendants, 1950.

Carnival Queen Kate Nixon is crowned while Audrey Booth (right) smiles approval. Hospital Saturday, 1936.

conducted the band, but didn't take it to contests. Dennis Heath from Foden's band did that, and later Teddy Gray, also of Foden's.

We did a lot of concerts, but we were at a disadvantage. Foden's had help from the company to buy uniforms and instruments, whereas the Biddulph Moor Band had to raise money purely by its own efforts.

By the Sixties we were in demand everywhere. We played at Congleton Carnival, the Pavilion Gardens at Buxton, the parks in Stoke-on-Trent and local schools. We charged £25 for two performances on Sunday afternoons and evenings in the park, and our repertoire included marches, hymns, overtures, classics, operettas - just about everything that could be transcribed for a band.

Once we were playing Rimsky Korsakov's Scheherazade at Belle Vue when I had a nose bleed half way through my cornet solo. By dint of good fortune I managed to struggle through to the end. On another occasion a bass player got into a panic before a contest, shouting he'd lost his glasses, until someone told him they were on top of his head. Then there was the time Norman Machin's slide fell off his trombone as he was announcing a piece. People got very nervous, especially when they had to do a solo. If they fluffed it they felt they'd let the entire band down.

Contests were held between different bands and different categories of bands in different areas. We were in the Third Section in 1958, but by 1969 we'd made it to the Premier Section. Contests were all day affairs, with as many as twenty bands taking part and examined by a panel of judges hidden behind a screen. Audiences were massive, and local radio would come along too. Competition was so fierce each band member had to be signed in to stop cheating by 'borrowing' a member from another band. We were practising up to the last minute, sometimes on the bus. London was the most prestigious venue of all.

We were pleased as punch when we had a record out. We'd just done a concert at Biddulph High School and Simon Penfold, a band fanatic from Radio Stoke, was there. We got the recording through Radio Stoke and it sold very well. That was in 1969.

Throughout the early '70s competition from bands like Royal Doulton became stronger. Not only that, but Teddy Gray went to conduct for them and took some of our best players with him. From that time the band began to go down.

We joined the Selectus Band as Greenway Selectus, but we never did as well again as we had in the '60s, and by the '80s the band was wound up. A sad fate when you consider other bands used to come to watch us perform'

Tommy

'I agree with Anne regarding sponsorship of the bands. Whereas Foden's and Black Dyke were given money by the firms because of the prestige they brought, we had to pay our own expenses. We even had to find 1/- a week for the privilege of being a band member, and there were constant meetings to discuss how to raise money for the band. At one stage we were set to buy the Miners' Welfare, but some members were against it when Selectus said they'd sponsor us. From then on it was downbank

Getting to the venues could be a problem too. We used Bill Hall's bus, from Rock End. Like most service vehicles of the time, it was freezing cold in winter and you had to fold your feet under you to try and keep warm, then go straight on stage and perform. He was a good bloke in many ways and his bus was the cheapest by far, so we carried on using him. His daughter Sarah was on the band's fund-raising committee.

Music was always in the blood in our family. I played for an army band in the war, and after the war I had an offer to join a band in New Zealand, which I had to decline. My sister Alice was a fine soprano and sang duets with her husband Simeon Beech - he was manager of the Co-op after Charlie Elkin. She had professional lessons and sang in the Wesleyan choir. Her daughters Hazel and Sylvia were good Church singers, too.

I suppose we got it from my father Ben, who played the cornet for a Derbyshire band before he came to Biddulph Moor. The band over there got him his job at Whitfield Colliery, but he volunteered for the army in the First War and got gassed. It never stopped him enjoying his music, though.'

While the Fletchers were busily engaged touring the country with the Greenway Moor Prize Band - the title 'Greenway' adopted from the name given to this area of Biddulph Moor a century ago and used to avoid confusion with Biddulph Band - Ailsa's father Joe Turner was involved in other aspects of local entertainment.

Ailsa

'My father came from Biddulph. At twelve he left school and went to live on a farm at Horton. He joined the army at seventeen and served in the Somme and Mons. He was commissioned because of his bravery and made Second Lieutenant. He was also the mace bearer and drummer in the army band. At the end of World War One he married a Horton girl and came to live on Biddulph Moor, where he stayed throughout his life. He was a committee member for Hospital Saturday and marshalled the parades dressed as a comic policeman.

He was a member and conductor of the Biddulph Moor Jazz Band, and a drummer in Greenway Moor Band for over thirty years; he also marshalled parades in Biddulph for Armistice Sunday. In later years he was a founder member of the Evergreen Club.'

Ailsa, wearing her mother's altered wedding dress, accompanies Alan in the 1928 Biddulph Moor Carnival.

Joe Turner wasn't alone in his commitment to village activities. The founder of Bailey's Shirt Factory, Aaron Bailey, was no stranger to the baton and under his tutelage village choirs flourished. School choirs came into being as a result of Headmasters Reeve's and Rogers' enthusiasm for music of all kinds, while church choirs sprang from equally enthusiastic congregations. As with the brass band, competition was a spur to excellence.

Ewart

'There were concerts all the time, held either in the Miners' Welfare or the Church Hall, (the old Infant School). They took in a lot of local talent, particularly the Biddulph Moor Girls' Choir, conducted by Aaron Bailey. My aunt was in the choir and I was told of their pride at winning a national singing competition in Wales. We were nearly all involved in music. At school I remember 'Dashing Away with the Smoothing Iron'. At one time the Headmaster, Mr Rogers, introduced the song 'Comrades in Arms' - *'It reminds me of a woman carrying twins'* he told the amused audience.

The Annual Co-op Concert took place at the Miners' Welfare. It was a variety show which gave local talent a chance to shine. I remember comedian Aaron Stanway, and a conjuror who swapped milk and confetti containers. Just as he got us confused he threw what we thought was milk over the audience. Predictably, it was confetti.

Hill Top and New Road Methodists produced excellent choirs and held camp meetings on Bailey's Hill, near the old quarry. Another church activity was Harvest Festival, held in a room above the Rose and Crown. The food was auctioned off to the highest bidder and the proceeds went towards a day's outing for older village people.

There were frequent excursions to mystery destinations in the '50s. The drivers were Frank Moss and Arthur Ball. I ran a yearly trip to York races, and church and chapel organised trips as far afield as Windsor and London. There was never an idle moment.'

It was not unusual for concert parties to be formed at the drop of a hat, as Jane Doorbar recalls.

Jane

'I founded our Church (Hill Top) concert party around 1960, and it went on for nearly twenty years. There were six of us women - me, Mrs Heathcote, Mrs Trinder, Mrs Chaddock, Mrs Armitt, Mrs Holland - and a lady from Horton Church told us they'd been let down for a concert - could we help? So we put on a concert, and it went from there. We often teamed up with Hill Top Glee Singers.

There wasn't much competition from television in those days, though Jane did acquire a set for the Queen's Coronation in 1953 and has fond memories of a young Anne Newton turning up at her house with her standard plea, *'It's nearly time for Children's Hour. Can I come in and watch?'* And when television was not available, there was the 'Scratch' or 'Bug hut' at Biddulph, where they showed three films a week and put on a Saturday Matinee, Biddulph Moor patrons making their way back by way of Nettlebeds track.'

However, it would be remiss in concluding this chapter not to mention an activity some would say was of ever greater importance - football. Arthur Barlow missed few matches during his time as a local policeman shortly after the War.

Arthur

'Bob Hassall kept the New Inn (now the Foxhound) before Jim Davies' departure. Bob was a keen footballer and we used to play in the field opposite his pub. Later, Sammy Stanway and his brothers Peter, Sid and Brian played, all talented footballers. When I finished in the Police Force in 1954, I gave it up for a time and became Secretary of the club instead. The Biddulph Moor team was really well known, and there was a full turn-out for every game. When Congleton or Leek saw the Whites advancing, they had to pull out all the stops.'

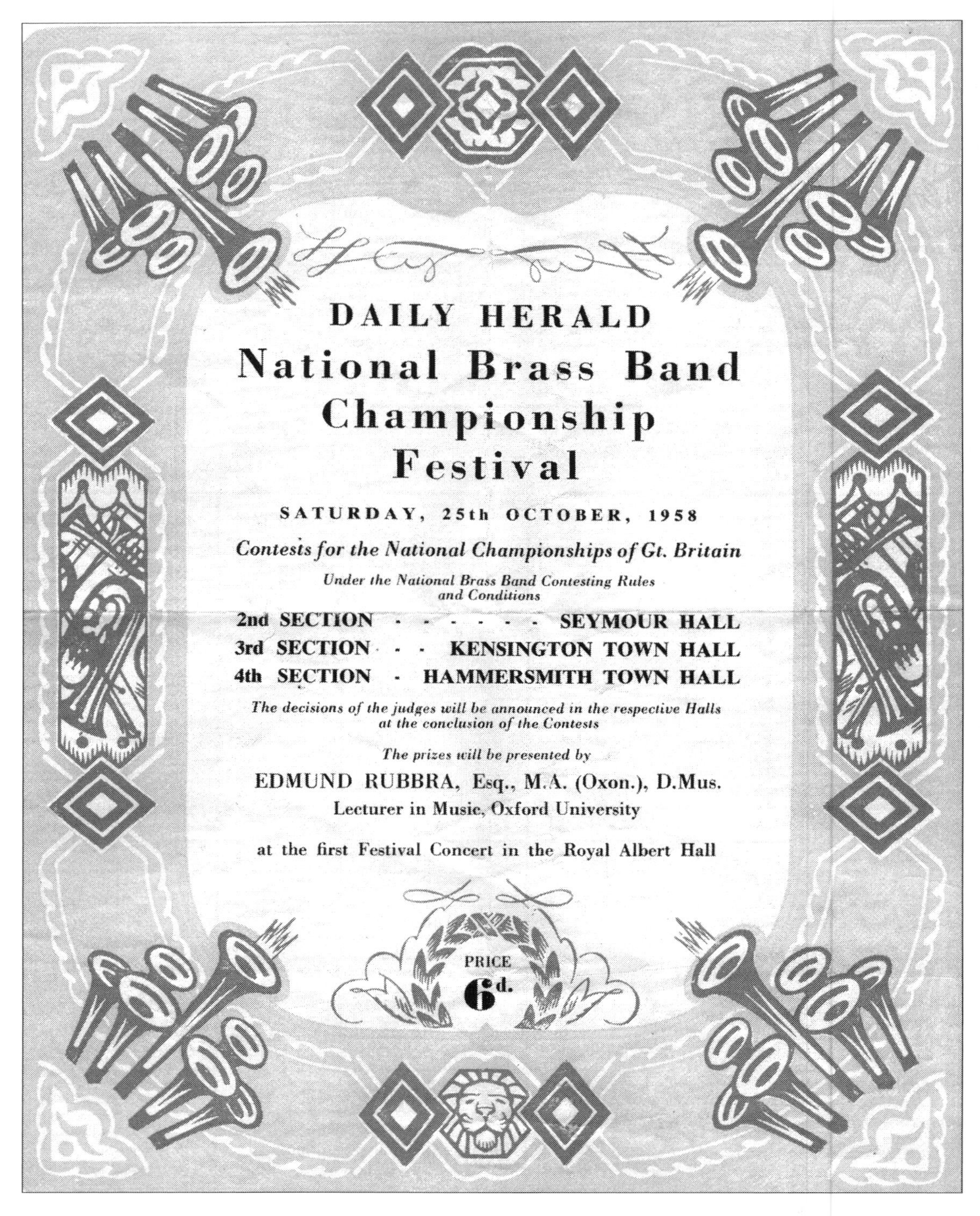

DAILY HERALD

National Brass Band Championship Festival

SATURDAY, 25th OCTOBER, 1958

Contests for the National Championships of Gt. Britain

Under the National Brass Band Contesting Rules and Conditions

2nd SECTION - - - - - - SEYMOUR HALL
3rd SECTION - - KENSINGTON TOWN HALL
4th SECTION - HAMMERSMITH TOWN HALL

The decisions of the judges will be announced in the respective Halls at the conclusion of the Contests

The prizes will be presented by

EDMUND RUBBRA, Esq., M.A. (Oxon.), D.Mus.
Lecturer in Music, Oxford University

at the first Festival Concert in the Royal Albert Hall

PRICE 6d.

Greenway Moor make a grab for the National Championships of Great Britain. The programme, 1958.

The band about to strike up in this Hospital Saturday picture, around 1900.

A proud band pose on the site of the Town Hall in Biddulph, 1960.

'As pleased as punch', Edward Gray conducting on the sleeve of the Greenway Moor Band's 1969 debut recording.

Below: Edward Gray, rehearsing Greenway Moor Band, 1962.

Jack Fletcher with proteges, early 1960s.

Members of band and choir pose for this 1950s picture, possibly in the Miners' Welfare.

Greenway Moor Prize Band turn for the camera, probably early 1960s.

Band at war. Taken in 1943 outside New Street Church air-raid shelter. Front, from left: Herbert Sherratt, George Beech, Arthur Bailey, Harry Beech. Middle, from left: Jack Fletcher, John Shufflebotham, Ben Fletcher, Harry Fletcher. Back: Percy Shufflebotham, Bill Beech, Frank Fletcher, Fred Machin, Jim Bailey, (?), Les Ash, Tom Beech.

The band raring to go, 1960.

Bandsmen strike up outside the Rose and Crown, 1930.

In full swing: band in the early 1960s.

Trophies in the bag for Greenway Moor Prize band, mid 1960s.

Jack Fletcher rehearsing the Junior Band, 1953.

Band rehearsals, 1952, at the Welfare. Jack Fletcher conducts.

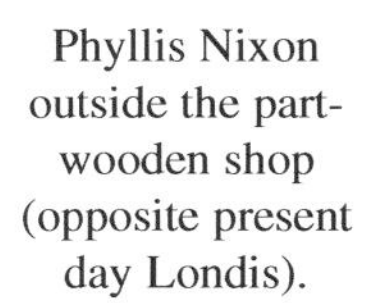

Phyllis Nixon outside the part-wooden shop (opposite present day Londis).

Polly Lovatt's store, Ridgefields, around 1960.

Below: Rose and Crown, around 1960.

Chapter 4
Bulging Bags

At the time I had to do a lot of paperwork, and looking through the school accounts I noticed Martha Ann Brown, the local shopkeeper, hadn't been paid for the cleaning materials she'd sent to the school over the last three years. Martha was a very nice, gentle woman, very polite. When I went to the shop to find out why, she said: 'I know they'll pay me in their own good time.' She didn't realise she had to complete an invoice for the Head Office at Stafford. I brought her a batch to fill in. She was owed £50 - a tidy sum in 1955!

Malcolm Locker, Teacher at Top School 1954-8.

When I arrived with the first rash of bungalows in 1965, the many shops which had once provided both a service and a living had been reduced to a handful. 'Florrie's' (now Village News) and the Spar, (now Londis) then run by Albert Newton, continued, occupying convenient central positions which were and still are beneficial to local trade. The Co-op, too, was in business. Phyllis and Harold Nixon still sold shoes from their Woodhouse Lane bungalow and you could buy your middle-cut from the local butcher. Newsagent Sidney Hulme - known affectionately as Sid 'Times' - had survived until then, and I was audacious enough to ask why the wall behind his counter was hidden under pasted sheets of newsprint. I forget his reply, but Sid was soon to join the rest, his Cottage Lane shop and shed demolished to make way for the new estate and Sid taking up residence in one of the new council-built bungalows alongside the Co-op. The butcher closed shortly after, and Phyllis and Harold ceased trading in 1989.

At the time of writing three village shops remain to provide an essential local service. Village News (Spar) and Londis (with Post Office) continue as General Stores. The old Co-op has been converted into a chemist's. At Robin Hill, Macclesfield Stone has built a sound reputation trading from what was once Wood's Grocery Stores.

It was a very different picture when Ewart Nixon was a lad.

Ewart

'Up until the late '50s there was a shop every few yards. Most were grocers, but there was a range of other shops too, enough to make the village self-sufficient in the basics. There were two grocers at Rock End alone - Taylor's and Lovatt's - and Wood's stores where Macclesfield Stone now trades. Then opposite the Miners' Welfare, Martha Ann Brown had her grocery. They all made a living.

Charlie Holland sold batteries and charged up accumulators for radio sets from one of the houses just up from Martha's, and Nixon's had the shop on the corner of Leek Lane and New Street. They baked bread and cakes and sold home-knitted garments, like jumpers. The Co-op was going strong too.

There were quite a few characters in those days. William Harold Plant always wore breeches because it was said he had designs on becoming a jockey. His shop was in Plant's

Biddulph Moor Schools
To Ann Finney for the quarter ending Sep 30th 1897

		£	s	d
	For sweeping big School	1	0	0
	Infants		13	
	Boy		6	6
Aug	scrubing School		6	
	towels & dusters		1	6
	Black lead & soap		1	6
Aug 18	one sweeping brush		2	6
	four weeks fire lighting		2	
	chips for fire lighting		1	
Sept	2 gallons of paraffin Oil		1	4
	lamp brush			6
		2	15	10

Received with thanks Oct 5th 1897 2.15.10 A Finney

School order placed with shopkeeper Ann Finney, 1897.

HIGH STREET,
Bradley Green, Dec 1st 1881.

Mr Rev H Gordon

Dr. to JOHN DAVENPORT,
Plumber, Glazier, House, Sign & Decorative Painter.
AUTHORIZED GAS AND WATER FITTER.

			s	d
1880 May 20th	1 qt linseed oil 1/- . 1 qt turps 1/- . 3 lb red @ /3		2	9
Sep 4th	Biddulph Moor School 4 sqrs @ 1/-		4	0
June 1881	1 qt linseed oil 1/-		1	0
			7	9

School order placed with Biddulph (Bradley Green) tradesman, 1881.

Yard, just below the Rose and Crown. Before it finally folded it had been a butcher's, a fish and chip shop, a sweet shop, a greetings' card shop and a hairdresser's.

The Co-op was the biggest and most modern of the shops. Goods could be purchased throughout the week and settled up on pay day. Where debt was incurred, payment was deferred until the dividend was due. That usually paid for the goods. There was also a Penny Bank. The Co-op also stocked wheat, barley and animal food for smallholders and farmers. The main warehouse was in Congleton to the rear of Mill Street. The bakery was attached, and bread was still warm when it was delivered to Biddulph Moor Co-op. Eighty-five per cent of Biddulph Moor people used the Co-op, and local shops bought goods from them in bulk and resold them in bits and drabs, claiming a dividend from the bulk buy.

The site now occupied by Village News was owned originally by Tom Bailey but known as 'Florrie's' after Florrie Bailey, who served there for years. Until the present shop was built it was just a hut, with a tin garage for the local bus next door. The vegetables sold there were supplied by Florrie's brother, who had Beckfield Farm.

Clem Simpson's butcher's shop (Clem's) was also a wooden shed. Later it became a shoe repair shop. It was on the site of the '50s Police House - now a private house - opposite Londis.

Above where Londis now stands was Miss Sherratt's Post Office, a bake-house which became a seconds' clothes shop owned by Amos Wilshaw and, on the corner of Ridgefields, a long demolished grocery run by Polly Lovatt. She also sold lamp oil and lamp glasses, since before the war many locals relied on lamps for their lighting.

There were other shops away from the village centre. In Church Lane Mrs Brown and her husband sold and repaired shoes and clogs, and there was a shed behind the house where haberdashery and buttons were sold. The sole petrol outlet was at Weathercock Farm, owned by Frank Shufflebotham. He also sold good second-hand furniture and delivered coal. Even Spout Lane had a grocery, owned by Mrs Beech.

Sidney Hulme (known locally as Sid 'Times') had his newsagent's in Cottage lane. He also sold mineral water, razor blades and cigarettes. He was a good musician and played regularly at the Rose and Crown. He practised on a pedal organ at home. Sid was quite a character, and one particular incident concerning him sticks in my mind. There was another Rose and Crown pianist, Peter Brough, who always played by ear using only the black notes. Leaning over the piano one night, Sid inquired, *'Are there no white notes on that piano, Pete?'* On another occasion Sid met Billy Booth, the local undertaker in the bar. *'Will you have one with me, Sid?'* Billy asked. *'Ay, but I'm not ready for you yet,'* came the reply. Sometimes Sid would go into the Rose and Crown without ever going up to the bar. He'd just put his money on the counter without saying anything. The landlord would put a Guinness on the bar and Sid would go and stand by the door and drink it, not a word spoken. He was no fool, just eccentric. He'd once taken a course in psychology and had a disagreement with his tutor over the meaning of some of the words used in the course. His argument proved successful by all accounts.

The Rose and Crown was run by Joe Murphy in the 1930s. It was always well patronised, but Joe wouldn't allow women in. The other shops I remember are a tuck shop which opened for a time after the War just below Top School, and Royal Shop serving the more outlying houses where Hot Lane joins Top Road. It sold paraffin for oil lamps and corn for poultry.'

BIDDULPH MOOR 1970s

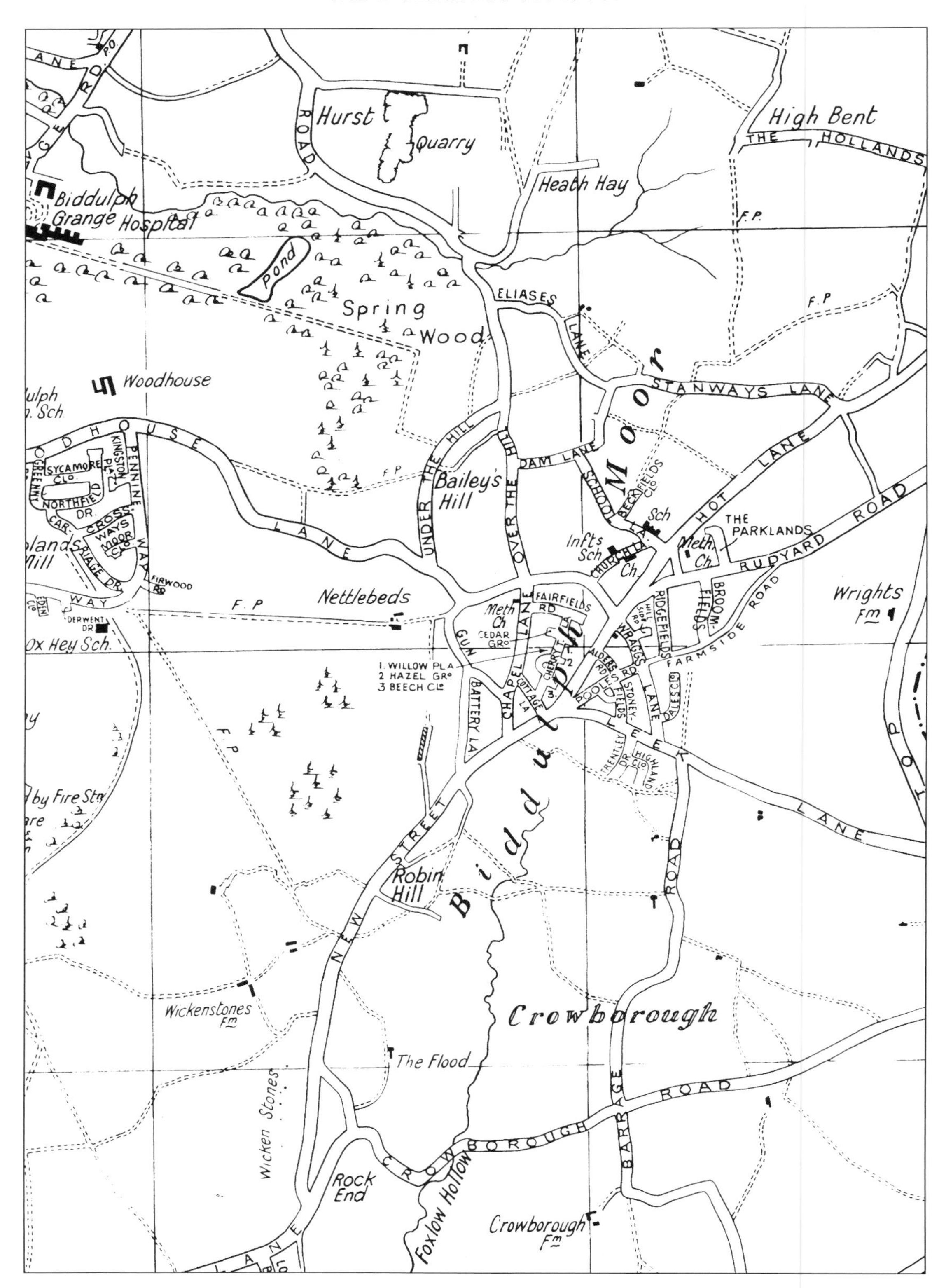

Ailsa

'You couldn't always afford new shoes, so cobblers were kept busy. I remember Stanway's, who worked from a wooden hut at Barn Farm next to Top School, Tom Beech's in Wragg's Lane and Holdcroft's in New Street.

Most of the farms would sell you a pound of cheese or butter, or a quart of milk. Then there was poultry, eggs and rabbit. Some toured with baskets of goods. Mr Proctor sold fruit and veg from a horse-drawn cart, later from a van. Sam Sherratt did the same. Mr Machin also toured the village with his horse and cart, selling bread and cakes, while Mr Elkin, Mr Shallcross and Mr Frost went from door to door selling clothes and wool. Undertaker Billy Booth made coffins, and later went into general joinery. His workshop was on the corner of Hot Lane and New Road (now Rudyard Road)

In the '50s milk delivery was by pony and trap. Isaac Brown was one of the last to do it that way. I believe he got his milk from a herd of Jerseys, which were a rare sight on the moor. Very creamy it was, too.'

Anne Newton remembers working in her student vacations for the Co-op, particularly the speed with which the manager could reckon up a column of figures using nothing more than his brain.

Anne

'They used to sell a lot of farmers' produce, grain and so on. The manager lived in the adjoining house at a nominal rent. At that time they were doing orders for locals, and delivering them by van. A lorry used to arrive at the shop at frequent intervals bringing fruit and vegetables from the wholesalers.'

Bob Pass served his apprenticeship as a joiner with Billy Booth just as the War started. Billy's business produced a wide range of products, including sheds, hencotes and greenhouses, but undertaking was his mainstay. By the time he was fifteen Bob was already making coffins on his own. Not long after he learnt to drive.

Bob

'I learnt by shifting the funeral cars in and out of the garage. One day one of the drivers didn't turn up, so Billy said *'Right, you're on a funeral this afternoon,'* and that was it. Billy was an excellent joiner and I learnt from him. His cars were kept where the garage is now (Rudyard Road). It was a big wooden structure. The workshop was upstairs where it is now, and he lived with his grandmother in the adjoining cottage.

The funeral business was hard work. You had some terrible jobs to attend to. There was no refrigeration then. People just died and you laid them out in their own home. You got used to it after a time.

Sometimes I would borrow a car from Billy Booth to fetch Fred and Harry Mortimer from Sandbach. They were members of Foden's Band, and they used to practice with the Greenway Moor Band upstairs at the New Inn (now the Foxhound). The band carried on during the war, but it was depleted because of call up. Miners formed the majority, because they were exempt.'

Between 1965 and 1989 Phyllis and Harold Nixon sold shoes and items of knitwear from their

Woodhouse Lane bungalow. Before that they had sold shoes at the wooden shop then situated opposite where Londis is now.

Harold

'A butcher, Sam Bailey, had the wooden shop originally. I remember him killing pigs on his farm, and I suppose they sold the pork at the shop. Later another butcher, Clem Simpson, owned it, but then he moved across the road. I believe Billy Clewes took over the butcher's business. He was followed by Harry Bailey's shoe business, and my brother took over from him. My brother Howard did shoes, shoe repairs and drapery. When he died, Phyllis and I kept the business going. The ground on which the wooden shop was built might have belonged to the county council. It was part of the plot where the Police Station was built in the '50s. I have an idea Joe Plant took the wooden shop down and rebuilt it up Rudyard Road as a farm shed.'

Phyllis

'When we moved to the bungalow we did a good trade in wellingtons. We did especially well at Christmas because we ran a club, so much a week, and put stuff away for the customers until then. That faded away, mainly because of cars and supermarkets.

We used to sell little toy cars and jumpers as well, and at Christmas we'd sell decorations. Once I had a decoration hanging up in the shop and someone brought that! We started to stock not only shoes but knitwear, cardigans and babywear - even ornaments.

I always remember Nicholas Triner used to buy little Matchbox toys, then come back a day or two later and say: *'Phyllis, I've had this one a bit. Can I change it now?'* I still remind him of it when I see him now.'

Harold

'There used to be shops all over the moor. Almost every need was met by somebody. There was even ice cream sold from a cart: Proctor's Pure Ices. And I believe they sold groceries up at Three Nooks Farm on Top road, right off the beaten track.

I have visual memories of Polly Lovatt's at the corner of Ridgefields. It was so packed you could hardly get through the door. It was dim inside, and you couldn't see anybody. Then a voice would come out of nowhere: *'Yes?'*

She used to pump paraffin for lamps from a big container which she kept next to the foodstuffs. Her husband Percy and her daughter worked there as well. Martha Ann Brown's was similar, stuff from floor to ceiling piled everywhere, grain, groceries, and a bacon hand-slicer stuck on the counter.'

Phyllis

'You had your local customers who stuck with you. I even had one man knocking me up at eleven o'clock at night for clothes. I think he'd just come back from the Rose and Crown. Then there was Sid 'Times', a right character. On one occasion someone saw Sid delivering a sack load of papers and asked: *'Can I buy a paper?' 'Ay,'* said Sid. *'You can have one if you want to get one from the shop.'*

Sid also had the habit of throwing papers at the door. He did it once as the door was being opened, and he accidentally hit the woman in the face. She wasn't best pleased.'

KELLY'S DIRECTORY BIDDULPH AND BIDDULPH MOOR 1863

BIDDULPH is a hilly moorland district, nearly 8 miles north-west of Leek, and above 2 South-east of Congleton station, 10 from Macclesfield, 11 from Newcastle, 7 from Burslem and from Hanley, 159 from London, 30 from Stafford, 60 from Birmingham, and 28 from Manchester, in the northern angle of North Pirehill hundred, Congleton union and county court district, North Staffordshire, and Lichfield diocese, Stafford archdeaconry, and Leek deanery. The Trent rises at the north end of the parish, under the high rocky ridge called Mole Cop, near the boundary between Cheshire and Staffordshire. The parish abounds in coal, has several large collieries and ironworks, several quarries of hard and durable stone, a scrap iron and spade and shovel manufactory, and a silk mill. The living is a vicarage, value £122, in the gift of James Bateman, Esq.; the Rev. William Henry Holt is the incumbent. The church of St. Lawrence is a neat structure, with an embattled tower and 5 bells, situated on the high road to the Potteries. At Knypersley is a district church with parsonage and school house, the sole cost (£10,000) having been borne by the late John Bateman, of Knypersley Hall; the Rev. James Metcalfe is the minister; it is in the Early English style, with a spire and 1 bell. The Wesleyan and Primitive Methodists have each two places of worship here. Knypersley Hall is the residence of Robert Heath, Esq. Biddulph Hall, situate at the north end of the parish, anciently the seat of the Biddulph family, has long been in ruins, except the north end, which is occupied by a farmer. A little further, on the borders of Cheshire, are the remains of a Druidical temple, called the Bridestones, consisting of eight upright freestones, two of which are within a semicircle formed by the other six. Near these stones are the remains of three curious caves, excavated in the solid rock. Biddulph is divided into four hamlets and manors, viz., Overton, of which Lord Camoys is the lord; Middle and Nether Biddulph, of which Capt. Mainwaring, R.N., is lord; and Knypersley, of which James Bateman, Esq., is lord. Here is a Free school, at Crabtree Green, endowed with £8 10s. yearly and the interest of £100. At Knypersley a new school has been lately opened, and very recently at Biddulph Moor another free school has been erected. The poor have the following annual benefactions:—28s. as the interest of £30 left by various persons; 28s. from £35, left in 1732 by John Stonier; and £4 10s. from £100, left in 1812 by William Carter. Five alms houses are now in the course of erection, raised at the cost of the parishioners of Biddulph, in memory of the late John Bateman, Esq. of Knypersley Hall. Biddulph Valley Railway station is here, a branch of the North Staffordshire line, connecting Congleton with Stoke, for the conveyance of minerals only. The acreage is 5,000. Bradley Green is in this parish. The North Staffordshire railway has a station at Mow Cop, 154 miles from London, 25 from Stafford, 54½ from Birmingham, 12¼ from Macclesfield, and 29¼ from Manchester. Gillow Heath is ½ a mile south-west.

PRIVATE RESIDENTS.

Bateman James, esq. M.A., F.R.A. Biddulph grange
Buckley Mr. Robert, Poolfold
Clive Henry, esq. Moor house, Biddulph valley
Gosling Samuel Francis, esq
Heath Robert, esq. Knypersley hall
Holland Mr. Ralph, Poolfold
Holt Rev. William Henry, M.A. [vicar]
Hulme William, esq. Bradley green
Metcalfe Rev. James, M.A. Knypersley
Sharnock Rev. James [curate]

COMMERCIAL.

Allcock Thomas, farmer & cheesefactor, Falls
Armitt Thomas, beer retailer
Ash Richard, farmer, Woodhouse farm
Bailey Isaac, beer retailer
Bailey Isaac, farmer & shopkeeper, Pool head
Bailey Matthew, farmer, Outward gate
Bailey Thomas, farmer, Ox hay
Bailey William, farmer, Nettle beds
Beales Robert, physician, Bradley green, & at Chapel street, Congleton
Beech Lot, farmer & tailor, Long edge
Birks George, farmer & brickmaker, Whitemore cottage
Booth Thomas, cowkeeper & shopkeeper
Bowers Thomas, farmer, Hill farm
Bradbury William, collier, Bradley green
Brassington Enoch, farmer
Brocklehurst John, farmer, New pool
Brough Ralph, farmer, New pool
Brown Charles, farmer, Dial lane
Brown Thomas, farmer, Dial lane
Bullock John, shopkeeper
Carter George, grocer, Bradley green
Carter Ralph, shoemaker, Pool fold
Carter Ralph, shoemaker
Chaddock William, farmer, Gillow heath
Challinor Samuel, farmer, Church farm
Cheetham Joseph, grocer & beer retailer, Bradley green
Compton Joseph, butcher
Walley James, butcher, Bradley green
Walley Jas. greengrocer, Bradley green
Walley Joseph, shopkeeper, Bradley green
Walley Simeon, brickmaker, Bradley green
Cotterill Jonathan, farmer, Whitemoor
Cotterill Thos. farmer, Biddulph house
Dale Benjamin, blacksmith, Dial lane
Delves Joseph, plumber & painter, Bradley green
Doorbar John, farmer, Meadow style
Doorbar Thos. *Wheel inn* & wheelwright
Embury Richard, wheelwright, Overton
Fellwright William, farmer, Hay hill
Furnival George, plumber, painter &c. Bradley green
Gater William, tailor
Gibson James, farmer, Hurst
Goodhall William, farmer, Moody stre e
Gosling & Myatt, coal masters
Gosling Samuel Francis, spade & shovel maker, ironmaster & bar iron manufctr
Gosling Saml. Francis, surgeon, Leigh ho
Hancock James, grocer & provision dealer, Gillow heath
Harding John, builder, Bradley green
Harrison William, farmer, Cross
Harthern William, silk throwster
Heath Robert, ironworks & colliery (John Paton, agt.), Biddulph valley
Heathcote Chas. farmer, Biddulph moor
Heathcote Joseph Felix, shopkeeper, Bradley green
Holland James, cowkeeper
Horn Ralph, farmer, Overton
Hulme Richard, grocer, Biddulph moor
Jervis William, stationer & bookseller, Bradley green
Johnson John, joiner, Bradley green
Kirk Rupert, farmer, Common
Lancaster Wm. grocer, Biddulph moor
Lawton Thomas, farmer, Bradley green
Lawton Thos. farmer & shoemaker, Moor
Leigh John, shopkeeper, Bradley green
Lockett John, builder, Marsh green
Lockett Richard, farmer, Marsh green
Lowe Sarah (Mrs.), *Talbot*
Mayor James, farmer & collier, Park
Mitchell Charles, farmer, Pool fold
Mitchell Thomas, timber mer. Pool fold
Moss John, shopkeeper
Walley John, butcher, Bradley green
Wark James Henry, schoolmaster & post office receiving house, Knypersley
Whitehurst Charles, farmer, Knypersley
Whitehurst John, farmer, Gillow heath
Whitehurst Thos. farmer, Gillow heath
Murfin Archibald, beer retailer, Biddulph moor
Myatt & Cotterill, millers, Bradley grn
Myott John, farmer, Hall
Myott Martha (Mrs.), farmer, Butter lands
Myott Richard, farmer, High Overton
Myott Richard, farmer, Lower Overton
Nixon Jonathan, cowkeeper & shoemkr
Oakes Elijah, shoemaker, Bradley green
Oakes John, shoemaker, Bradley green
Oakes Samuel, grocer & provision dealer
Partington Thomas, school & parish clerk
Paton John, agent to the Biddulph valley ironworks, Biddulph valley
Penkethman Thomas, shopkpr. Pool fold
Phillips Thomas, tailor, Bradley green
Pierpoint Richard, farmer, Park
Plant Enoch, *New inn*, Biddulph moor
Plant James, miller, Mill bank
Plant John, farmer, Firewood house
Plant William, farmer, Gate
Pointer William, joiner & wheelwright, Biddulph moor
Rowley Simeon, linendraper, Bradley grn
Ryder James, blacksmith
Ryder Thomas, farmer, Beacon house
Shaw Solomon, farmer, Marsh green
Sherratt Charles, sen. farmer, Knypersley end
Sherratt Charles, jun. farmer, Braddocks hays
Sherratt Cicely, shopkeeper
Sherratt George, china dlr. Bradley grn
Sherratt Jane (Mrs.), dairy, Knowle style
Sherratt John, farmer
Shufflebotham James, farmer, Beech flds
Smith Thomas, farmer, Knypersley park
Smith William Barnet, wood turner, Biddulph moor
Stonier John, assistant overseer & collector of taxes
Stonier William, timber merchant
Taylor Thomas, blacksmith, Knypersley
Thorn James, shopkeeper, Bradley grn
Turnock John, farmer, Dirty lane
Wilding Martha (Mrs.), shopkeeper, Bradley green
Williams John, *Church House hotel*
Williams John A. chemist & druggist
Wilshaw William, farmer & beer retailer, Bradley green

POST OFFICE.—James Henry Wark, receiver, Knypersley. Letters arrive from Congleton 9·30 a.m.; dispatched at 5 p.m

Parish School, Crabtree green, James Partington, master
Free School, Biddulph moor, Joseph Hall, master
National School, Knypersley, James Henry Wark, master; Mrs. Hannah Knight Wark, mistress

One of the Invincibles poses by bus garage opposite Rose and Crown, probably early 1930s.

Dodge wagon, early 1930s. Snape's Coal and Milk retailers, Park Lane.

Guy bus, 1922. Driver Ailsa's father Joseph Turner on step, James Bailey looking out.

Below:
Pride of the fleet: Biddulph and District Motors, founded in 1934.

Chapter 5
From Pillar to Post

When a service started, they ran a bus to Leek every Wednesday for the market. Women used to wait for it at the farm gate with their baskets of eggs and butter, and even a chicken or two. Then they started a special bus on Saturdays to Tunstall Market. I used to walk to the Post Box to get it.

Jane Doorbar, recalling the first buses to Biddulph Moor in the 1920s.

There were hardly any cars in the village. I remember the Rev. Fletcher had one, and the Co-op manager had another, though there might have been one or two on the outlying farms and, of course, the medical services had their own transport.

Ken Pointon, recalling what he was told about Biddulph Moor in the 1930s

Until the early '20s, when a regular bus service to Biddulph Moor began, you either walked, cycled, or hitched a lift on a cart. Horse-drawn carts were the only vehicles capable of negotiating the holed and pitted roads which linked isolated farms and hamlets at that time.

The growing popularity of the internal combustion engine in the years following the Great War seems to have preceded tarmaced roads in many rural areas, and according to Jane Doorbar even when the bus service began it was not unusual, particularly in winter, for a bus to be *'up to the axles in mud and holes'*.

The problem was solved when New Street was tarmaced, thereby making a more-or-less accurate bus timetable possible for the first time. Particularly welcome was the upgrading of the stretch outside the Co-op, which had taken the brunt of delivery vans and carts since its opening in 1922 with predictable results underfoot.

Jane

Before the buses we walked for miles and never thought anything of it. I remember my mother walking to Tunstall to listen to a choir at the Jubilee Chapel, then starting back at 8pm to get home before midnight because the Wells' bus had broken down at Brindley Ford. And I clearly remember my brother walking from Stoke Station to our house when he was on leave (from World War I). We were a bit long getting to the door, and he said if we didn't open up he was going back to the fighting!

As children we also walked from school to home for dinner, because my mother said we'd get into mischief if we stayed at school in the lunch break.

Ailsa Booth has a personal interest in the inauguration of the bus service to Biddulph Moor: her father Joseph Turner was one of the first drivers.

Ailsa

My father learnt to drive in the army during the First War. When it finished he found employment with Peter Stanway, who owned a charabanc garaged on Top Road off Leek Lane. After that he went to drive for Sam Bailey, who had a garage near Hope House in

Wragg's Lane. Father also learnt mechanics in the army, and worked on the engines as well as doing repairs and cleaning. By the early '30s Sam had merged with the Invincibles and my father began to work for them. Their garage was by Florrie's Shop (now Village News, Spar). My father-in-law Albert Booth was a bus conductor for them, and one of the directors of the company. Another director and driver was Sidney Buckley.

Another merger took place in 1934, when a new company was formed called Biddulph and District Motors Ltd. They acquired the old Invincible garage as well as their own garage in Biddulph where the library is now. In 1936 they sold out to Northwestern. The first foreman was Dennis Sherratt, who died in 1950. My father took over from him and remained there until 1960, when he retired. The same year the garage was closed and new ones built in Walley Street, Biddulph. Later, Northwestern sold out to PMT.

One name I recall from that time is Marjorie Proctor, a conductress. She met William Hooper, a soldier in the 1939/45 War stationed on the moor, and they got married. The marriage lasted until his death quite recently. Fares after the War were 2d to Biddulph one way, and 4d to Congleton.

Like Jane, Ailsa has vivid memories of the Market Day bus to Leek.

Ailsa

There were two routes, one via Biddulph Park, Long Edge and Rushton; the other through Lask Edge, Blackwood Hill, Gratton, Horton and Rudyard. Passengers waited on their doorsteps with their sales goods - hens, ducks, rabbits in wicker cages and boxes which were loaded on the back of the bus. Sometimes the aisle was jammed with baskets of cheese, eggs, vegetables, jam - anything that would sell. My brother and me were sometimes given a present, a rabbit or a fantail pigeon, because my dad (the driver) had helped the passengers load and unload their goods. The other occasion I remember is the time of the Coronation, 1953, when they ran a bus which had been decked out and decorated to Biddulph Moor. It was beautifully done.

The Rev Fletcher, Rector of Christ Church from 1920 to 1947, was one of the few fortunate enough to own a private car. His chain-driven Trojan, a common sight in the village, can still be pictured by Ewart, Ken and Bob, and the job of simple servicing fell to the Bob.

Bob

The Rector was quite well off in those days. He was able to employ a servant and a gardener who'd look after the church boiler as well. I got on quite well with the Rector. I used to do a bit of chauffering for him. He had an old Trojan car with a twin cylinder engine under the seat. The plugs used to oil up as they do with 2-stroke engines, but he'd only let me take them out and clean them once in a while. He wouldn't let me do anything else. If something big went wrong he'd have the company's mechanics down from Yorkshire - the men in white overalls.

The lamp was presented to the Rev. J. Sherratt's wife at the end of his Hill Top ministry, 1953.

New Street Church: outing to Trentham Gardens, late 1950s.

Presentation of chair to Hezekiah Beech, in recognition of his services to New Street Church, 1947.

Chapter 6
Sunday Bells

I remember once when a funeral tea was being provided at the church and milk had not been ordered for some reason. I rushed home to fetch a cow from the field, milked it and carried the milk back to the church in a jug just in time for the tea.

The late Mary Chaddock, recalling Hill Top Methodist Church in the '30s, and later recounted in the church's centenary booklet.

For many years we (Wesleyans) shared with Primitive Methodists two camp meetings each summer, when we processed from each chapel to unite on Bailey's Hill. There would be three preachers, and strains of such hymns as 'We're marching to Zion' would fill the air.

from the New Road Methodist Church centenary publication, compiled by Annie Holland

My two younger brothers and myself went to Sunday School at Christ Church at 9.30am. The teacher was Mr Reeve, who was also the Headmaster of the school and a lay preacher in the church. We later went to church for Morning Service at 10.15am, then Sunday School at 2.30pm, and as we got older, Evening Prayers at 6.30pm.

The late Annie Ethel Cook recalling Sundays at Christ Church in the 1920s, from her reminiscences *My Childhood Memories on the Moor*

That Biddulph Moor should boast three substantial places of worship (four, if Lask Edge Chapel were included) is testimony to the faith of those who sought to address the spiritual needs of an earlier generation. It is hardly surprising that Methodism should have found a welcome home here, when one considers that the founding father of the Primitive Church, Hugh Bourne, had been raised in the area, and that John Wesley himself preached in The Hurst - his host William Stonier later becoming a member of the Biddulph Moor Society.

Neither was Biddulph Moor short of influential benefactors. James Bateman not only provided capital for the school (1852), but made a substantial contribution towards the building of Christ Church, which opened its doors to Anglican worship in 1863.

There had been more modest places of worship as the movement towards religious revival gained pace. Harold Nixon can recall mention of an early chapel at the Hollands, and around 1818 a Wesleyan Chapel at Beckfields was in use. Thirty five years later, land on Biddulph Moor had been released - again by James Bateman - for the building of a chapel to be used by members of the Primitive Methodist Connection. This basic building was replaced in 1869 by a second chapel at Under-the-Hill, long since converted into a cottage, and later, in 1904, by the more capacious and convenient Hill Top Methodist Church. The Wesleyans also sought to accommodate their growing numbers in a more central location, and this led to the establishment, in 1888, of the New Road Methodist Church.

Meanwhile the Anglicans had moved from Sunday Worship at the National School to Christ Church across the road. The gradual evolution of disparate dwellings into a nuclear village was thus reflected in these ambitious projects.

It is not the aim of this book to look into the history of the various religious movements, though it might be useful to point out that the Primitive and Wesleyan Societies amalgamated into the Methodist Church in 1932. Suffice it to say it took men and women of vision, generosity and conviction to ensure the various schemes came to fruition, and that through them many aspects of village life prospered.

Smiling Hill Top Sunday School Queen. Date unknown.

Jane Doorbar first attended Sunday School at Hill Top Church as a three-year-old in 1915, and still has her Sunday School prize from that date.

Jane

'I recall hearing of an incident years ago when a man who had previously been the worse for drink was converted. *'Do you believe Jesus turned water into wine?'* the Preacher thundered. *'He could do more than that,'* came the reply. *'He could turn it into food and furniture, since I bought neither before but spent it all on drink.'*

The Preachers were full of fire at that time. And you couldn't say anything at Sunday School, for no talking was allowed. On the other hand there was no shortage of events we looked forward to, especially singing and nativity plays, and later on, Women's Own. In fact I was the Chair of Women's Own for many years and we raised a good sum for the Church. I was also a Sunday School teacher in my twenties. The children used to call me Aunty Jane. Music was always to the fore. In the Sixties we founded the Ladies' Concert Party. The Hill Top Glee Singers began with twelve men.

Smiling Hill Top Sunday School Queen. Date unknown.

Part of an annual report of the educational and financial health of Biddulph Moor School and the Church - see also page 10..

GRANTS AND SUBSCRIPTIONS

TO THE

BIDDULPH MOOR CHURCH BUILDING & ENDOWMENT FUNDS

UP TO DECEMBER, 1862.

	£	s.	d.
James Bateman, Esq., for Endowment Fund	1000	0	0
The Lichfield Church Building Society, for Building Fund	200	0	0
The Incorporated Church Building Society, for ditto	175	0	0
Proceeds of Biddulph Moor Church Bazaar	132	6	9
Proceeds of the Grange Garden Tickets at the Biddulph Volunteer Review	104	12	0
The Rt. Hon. Lord Egerton of Tatton	100	0	0
Mrs. Stanier, Madely Manor, Newcastle-under Lyme	100	0	0
Rev. J. Brierley, Mossley Hall, Congleton	50	0	0
H. H. Williamson, Esq., Greenway Bank, Tunstall	50	0	0
T. Rowley, Esq., London	30	0	0
W. H. Ainsworth, Esq., Moss Bank, Bolton	25	0	0
Miss Sparrow, Bishton Hall, Rugeley	20	0	0
Rev. J. Brierley, (2nd donation)	20	0	0
Proceeds of Mow Cop Bazaar	20	0	0
The Lord Bishop of Lichfield	10	0	0
Rev. Francis Gordon, Moor Parsonage	10	0	0
Mrs. Kinnersley, Clough Hall, Kidsgrove	10	0	0
Miss Wathen, Biddulph Grange	10	0	0
S. F. Gosling, Esq., Lea House, Biddulph	10	0	0
J. B. Thorpe, Esq., Manchester	10	0	0
Collected on Moor Church Ground at Commemoration Meeting	9	0	0
Sermon at Biddulph Parish Church	5	11	5
Rev. W. Melland, Rushton Parsonage	5	5	0

	£	s.	d.
Mr. Yardley, Rushton Spencer	5	0	0
R. Wilbraham, Esq., Rode Heath	5	0	0
Rev. S. Bradshaw, Basford Hall, Leek	5	0	0
Mr. R. Myott, Higher Overton, Biddulph	5	0	0
— R. Myott, Lower Overton, Biddulph	5	0	0
Rev. W. Foster, Horton Parsonage, Leek	5	0	0
A Friend, by Mrs. Bateman, Biddulph Grange	5	0	0
C. Sewell, Esq., Manchester	5	0	0
Late Miss Frances Sewell, Manchester	5	0	0
G. H. Ackers, Esq., Moreton Hall	5	0	0
Sermon at Horton Church, Leek	3	0	0
Miss Selby, Biddulph Grange	2	2	0
Mess. Warrington & Sheldon, Congleton	2	2	0
Charles Harris, Esq., London	2	2	0
Mrs. Thorpe, London	2	0	0
Mr. Goode, Congleton	2	0	0
Mrs. Hutton, Congleton	2	0	0
Messrs. Miles and Brunt, London	1	10	0
Mr. Burghope, Congleton	1	1	0
— Webb, Congleton	1	1	0
Captain Jones, R.N., London	1	1	0
Two Friends, London	1	0	0
Rev. M. Brock, Bath	1	0	0
Mr. Woolley, Congleton	1	0	0
Messrs. Aston, Congleton	1	0	0
Mr. Braddock, by Mrs. Myott, Higher Overton	1	0	0
Thomas Livsey, Esq., London	1	0	0
George Livsey, Esq., London	1	0	0
Francis Merritt, Esq., London	1	0	0
Joseph Kimpton, Esq., London	1	0	0

THE METHODIST CHURCH

BIDDULPH CIRCUIT

Plan & Directory

JULY 6th, 1969 —— SEPTEMBER 30th, 1969

MINISTER'S MESSAGE

BIDDULPH AND MOW COP CIRCUIT will operate as from September and I welcome Rev. G. Brian Westwood as my colleague. Preachers appointed in September have been arranged by the Superintendents who are involved in this change of boundaries, therefore the name of Mr Westwood and myself will appear on other plans in addition to this issue.

The members of the Q.M. expressed their gratitude to Sister Edna for her tireless work at Park Lane, also among the young people and W.W. Preachers who have served on the former Circuit will no longer belong to the new Circuit, but we should like to say "Thank You" for all dedicated service in the past.

The Lord gave the Word . . .
Great was the company of the preachers . . .

No writer can describe their mission better than we find in the Holy Book :

> How beautiful are the feet of them that preach the Gospel of peace, and bring glad tidings of good things. Their sound is gone out into all lands and their words unto the ends of the world . . .

The Officers of Congleton (Wagg Street), Congleton (Kinsey Street), Mow Cop Churches will join our brethren on July 23rd to discuss policy and appoint Officers for the new Circuit.

Greetings to all the sick at home and in hospital.

Yours sincerely,

F. WILLCOX.

Marked New Plan Dates · 1969 · October 13·14 · November 9·30 · December 14·21

G S. Hagston, Printer, Biddulph. Phone 2190

Plan and Directory, Biddulph Methodist Circuit, 1969.

New Wesleyan Chapel,
BIDDULPH MOOR.

THE OPENING SERVICES

WILL BE HELD AS FOLLOWS:—

On Wednesday, April 4th, 1888,

A Tea Meeting

Will be held at Five o'clock; Tickets, 1s. each. At Seven o'clock,

A SERMON

Will be preached by

W. SHEPHERD ALLEN, Esq.,

OF WOODHEAD HALL, CHEADLE.

On Sunday, April 8th,

TWO SERMONS

Will be preached by

JAMES LOCKETT, ESQ.,

OF NORTON, NEAR BURSLEM; AT 2-30 and 6, p.m.
In the Evening, Silver will be thankfully received at the door.

On Monday, April 9th,

TWO SERMONS

Will be preached by the

REV. THOMAS CHAMPNESS,

OF ROCHDALE, Editor of "Joyful News," &c.; at 3-30 and 7, p.m. At 5 o'clock,

A TEA MEETING

WILL BE HELD; TICKETS, 1s. EACH.

A COLLECTION will be made after each Sermon, which with the profits of the Tea Meetings, will go to the Building Fund of the above New Chapel.

R. W. Clarson, Printer, "Mercury" Office, Congleton.

Inauguration of services at New Street Church, 1888.

The leading event of the year was the anniversary. We sang special anniversary hymns and there were processions on Sunday morning. On Monday night children sang and gave recitals. We used to walk down New Street, but there were camp meetings at Bailey's Hill.

One big event in the history of Hill Top Church was when we bought the Miners' Welfare Building at the end of Gun Battery Lane for use as a Sunday School and Youth Centre. It had been built in 1935 to provide better facilities than the old wooden Workingmen's Club adjacent to the Co-op building, but it never seemed to do well despite its bowling green and what have you. We paid over £1200 for it in 1951, but a lot of work had to put in to make it sound, including building buttresses to take the weight of the roof because the walls were weak.

It did really well and was used for wedding receptions, concerts, parties, crowning the Sunday School Queen and as a practice room for Greenway Moor Band. Later it was hired by the Scouts and as a Youth Club. At one time the Child Welfare Clinic was held there, but the building of the Village Hall in 1969 meant it began to fall out of use. It was sold and later converted into a private house, the proceeds going towards improving the facilities at Church.

I was very involved in the Church. After being a Sunday School teacher, I became a superintendent. There would be about 80 scholars. I opened up in the mornings and my sister in the afternoons. I was also a caretaker for a spell, and in the bad winter of 1963 I went for thirteen weeks getting coke in and ashes out because everything was freezing up.'

Good Friday Service, New Street Church, 1963. Rev Robert Tyreman.

Marian Flynn's father Hezekiah Beech, a former trustee of New Road Methodist Church and Sunday School Secretary, received an unexpected gift when in 1947 he was presented with a fireside chair in recognition of his half-century of service to the Wesleyan Church. One of a family of stonemasons long known for their craftsmanship, his son John trained to become a Methodist Minister at Handsworth College. Marian's late husband, too, was a local preacher.

Marian

'A minister has to train for about three years now. Even local preachers need to do exams, which they didn't at one time. But they used to be wonderful preachers, and they really lived out what they preached in their everyday lives.

We were separate from Hill Top until 1969, with the two churches on different circuits. Now we're on the same circuit. We have always shared the same beliefs, but Wesley founded the Wesleyan Church and William Clowes the Primitives.

My father Hezekiah was eighty-six when he died, and he kept his faith to the end. He built Mabel Triner's house, where I was born. His work and his religion were very important to him.

I always remember the Church being very active. There were outings to places like Trentham Gardens, and there were a lot of village carnivals. Sunday worship sometimes went on for most of the day, and on Good Friday there was tea between the services for anyone who wanted to stay on or for people who couldn't come in the afternoon.

I was at New Road Church until I moved away from the village. In 1954, I worshiped at Dane-in-Shaw, then in 1964 I married and moved back to Biddulph Moor and started at New Road again. The '50s were an especially happy time. We were all one big family and we all looked forward to worship, with services in the morning, at 3pm and again at 6pm. There was also a Sunday School in the afternoon and a prayer meeting on a Tuesday evening. Usually, around half a dozen attended. Previous to that there were prayer meetings on Sundays before morning service.

Wednesday evenings were taken up with the Wesley Guild, following Devotional and Christian Service themes. There were also meetings once a month held around the fire in the vestry, and these could be very well attended.

There were always treats for the younger Sunday School members once a year. We used to hold games in the farm at Ridgefields opposite where Polly Lovatt's shop used to be, and she'd supply us with refreshments like bread and ham for sandwiches to keep us all going.

The war curtailed a lot of that. In fact they built an air-raid shelter inside the Church grounds, near the back gate.

Music was important to us. There had been a choir for as long as I can remember, and after the War among the organists and pianists was Elizabeth Booth, Joseph Bailey, Cyril Beech and Robert Shufflebotham. Conductors were John and Robert Shufflebotham, Albert Copeland and Jack Fletcher. The Preacher chose the hymns, similar to those sung in the Anglican Church.

I remember it all with great affection.'

From the start, the rectors of Christ Church were involved in all that went on in the school opposite, and lessons were imbued with a strong Christian ethos. Biddulph Moor School Log for October 9th, 1873, records: *'This morning the Rector (Francis Gordon) took the class for a scripture lesson. They were not attentive to him and were reproved by the mistress after he left the school'.* The Rev Gordon's successors, whether or not they were better able to interest their disaffected charges, continued to work closely with pupils throughout the years, as well as taking a central role in village life. Although the Revs Sparling, Blackmore, Whieldon, Fletcher and Withington - whose collective ministries extended from 1884 to 1951 - appear regularly in the School Logs and reported village events, it is the Rev Fletcher's ministry (1920 to 1947) and that of the Rev Withington (1947-1951)which is chiefly recollected by Anglican parishioners Bob Pass and Mary Pointon.

Rev Fletcher, Rector of Christ Church 1920-47, and wife. Late 1930s.

Mrs Fletcher with sons Eric and Cecil, 1930.

Bob

'I got on well with the Rev Fletcher. His wife was a nice person, but she kept herself pretty much to herself. She'd come into the Church by the vestry door and sit by the organ. That's about all you'd see of her. They had two sons, but I never saw a lot of them because they were at college or school. One went into the Church like his father, and the other became a schoolmaster.

They lived in the old Rectory. The present Rectory (rented out by the Church at the time of writing) stands on the site of

Christ Church Bible Study Group, 1950. Rev Withington (Rector 1947-51) centre.

Rev Blackmore and daughter Dorothy, 1902-5.

Original sketch for Biddulph Moor Church and Parsonage, instigated no doubt by James Bateman. The present more modest Church was eventually built, and a separate Rectory constructed.

DEATH OF THE VICAR OF HORTON

Rev. Edwin Wheeldon's 14 Years' Work

We deeply regret to record the death, which occurred in his 65th year, of the Rev. Edwin Wheeldon, who has been Vicar of Horton, near Leek, for the past 14 years.

Mr. Wheeldon appeared in his usual health on Sunday, when he officiated at Holy Communion in the morning, and also conducted Matins. After lunch he went for a walk in the fields with his son, Mr. E. R. C. Wheeldon and, on returning, retired to his study to rest before Sunday School. A few

Rev Wheeldon, Rector Christ Church 1905-1920

a tennis court which was very popular in the '30s with competitions with Biddulph St Lawrence and Knypersley Church.

The Rev Fletcher didn't retire when he left Christ Church. He went to Wem and retired there. He'd be in his sixties when he left Biddulph Moor. His son went to Shrewsbury as a vicar.

Then the Rev Withington took over the Church. He was a really good man, with some original ideas. At one point he introduced an amplified recording of a peal of bells. I put the speakers up in the bell tower. Knypersley and Biddulph both had a peal of bells, but Biddulph Moor only had the one, so I suppose he thought the recording would keep us up to the mark. Unfortunately they turned out to be a bit of a disaster.

Nevertheless he was a very likeable man, and popular in the village. He moved on to Whitby after a few years, and the Rev Goode succeeded him.

When John McGuire (1971-2000) arrived he did a lot of work getting information on the old graveyard. One of the problems was there were a lot of graves with no one buried in them. They were sold to families, but you'd find the families buried virtually together in corners.'

Mary Pointon remembers the Rev Fletcher as *'someone special'*.

Mary

'He was a nice man, very straight and tall as you'd imagine a minister to be. He had a car called a Trojan. You looked up to him, and if he said anything you wouldn't contradict him. His son used to come back to the Church every so often. He died not long ago. He was very much like his father.

The Rev Fletcher's wife was tall, just like him. She used to come into Church by the vestry door and went out the same way. She always wore long clothes, and looked like a lady. I can't remember her speaking to anybody, and I can't say I knew his sons when I was young.

We used to have a Sunday School treat and go to different places because there wasn't anything else. Sometimes we were allowed in the Rectory grounds, and we used to play on a swing tied to one of the big trees.

Everything revolved around Church. We'd go morning, afternoon and night. The choir was always full, and some choristers like Cynthia Brassington and Muriel Rodgers still sing there. I can't remember there being a queen, as they had in the Methodist Church, but in other ways it was similar, such as going to Sunday School.

In my time Miss Reeve was the Sunday School teacher, and we had classes in what is now the Church Hall. She used to give you little Bible sayings on card for you to take home and learn for next time.

After Rev Fletcher left, the Rev Withington came. He was a very jovial man who'd go into the pub and have a drink with the villagers, the complete opposite to Rev Fletcher. But they were both excellent in their own ways.'

Tender for the Building of the New Church at Biddulph Moor

To the Committee of the Biddulph Moor Church

Gentlemen

The following is my tender for the Building Erecting and finishing the New Church at Biddulph Moor according to Plan and Specifications given (Viz) Excavating, draining, getting stone, Carting, Stone Masoning Building Tileing Lime and Sand Bricklaying Plastering Carpenters & Joiners work Plumbing & Glazing Painting Iron founding and Bell & fittings

	£	s	d
If Built with Zigzag Stone for the sum of	1120	10	0
If Built with hammer dressed Stone the sum of	1180	10	0

The work to be done in a substantial firm and plain Manner The Pulpit, Communion Table & Railing are not included in this tender for this reason The Revd T Gordon objected to the Plan of the same

As Witness My hand Joseph Stanway
Biddulph Moor

Joseph Stanway's tender for the building of Christ Church.

Rev Sparling, Rector Christ Church 1884-1902, with family and servants.

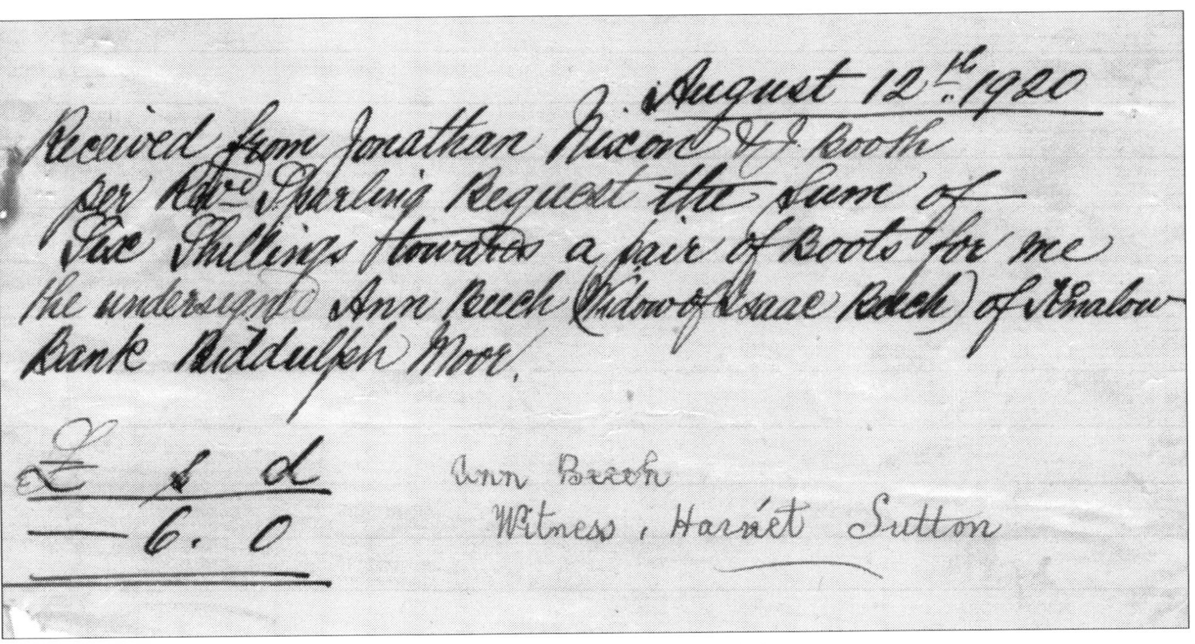

August 12th 1920

Received from Jonathan Nixon & J Booth per Revd Sparling Bequest the sum of Six Shillings towards a pair of Boots for me the undersigned Ann Beech (Widow of Isaac Beech) of Knalow Bank Biddulph Moor.

£	s	d
	6.	0

Ann Beech

Witness, Harriet Sutton

Rev Sparling bequest - a grateful recipient.

Christ Church: outing to Trentham Gardens, with members of Lask Edge Chapel. Probably early 1950s.

Ecclesiastical District of Christ Church. Biddulph Moor Biddulph

NAME	DATE	£	s.	d	SIGNATURE
Bailey Peter	August 10th 1917		7	6	her × mark
Beech Ann	" " "		7	6.	ann beech
Biddulph Emma	" " "		7	6	her × mark
Bould Eliza	" " "		7	6	her × mark.
Brown Charles	" " "		7	6.	his mark.
Cotterill Hugh	" " "		7	6.	her × mark.
Finney Ann	" " "		7	6.	her × mark.
Goldstraw Rachel	" " "		7	6	M J Beech
Holland Hannah	" " "		7	6	her × mark
Nixon Ellen	" " "		7	6.	her × mark
Nixon Edward	" " "		7	6.	S Shufflebotham
~~Nixon Henry~~	" " "				
Plant Harriet	" " "		7	6.	Harriet Plant
Pyatt Hannah	" " "		7	6.	her × mark.
Smart Charles	" " "		7	6	Sarah A Smart
Plant Mary Ann	" " "		7	6.	her × mark.
Stanway Mary	" " "		7	6.	Mary Stanway
Shorley Harriet	" " "		7	6	H Shorley
Wood George	" " "		7	6.	Ellen Wood
Simpson Lois	" " "		7	6.	her × mark.
Willshaw Thomas	" " "		7	6.	Mrs Willshaw
Shufflebotham Jonathan	" " "		7	6	Mrs S Shufflebotham
Bailey Harriet	August 10th 1917		7	6.	Harriet Baily
Battersby Fanny	" " "		7	6.	her × mark.
Byron Jane	" " "		7	6.	her × mark
Lancaster Theodosia	" " "		7	6.	her × mark
Lancaster Phoebe	" " "		7	6	her × mark
Lancaster Ruth	" " "		7	6	R Lancaster
Pass Abraham	" " "		7	6	A Pass
Pyatt Lucy	" " "		7	6.	Lucy Pyatt
Shenton Jane	" " "		7	6	her × mark
Shufflebotham Elizabeth	" " "		5	6	E Shufflebotham
Shufflebotham Elizabeth	" " "		7	6	E Shufflebotham

Recipients of the Rev Sparling's bequest, 1917.

Biddulph Moor Home Guard - with additional Biddulph recruits, 1941. Billy Booth front row, second left.

Chapter 7
The Moor at War

A very heavy air raid occurred last night. The objective seemed to be Liverpool and Manchester. Biddulph Moor was in the main path of the raiders and at least one heavy bomb fell on the village. As the raid was very prolonged, attendance suffered very considerably, with 58 absentees, representing only 63% attendance.
Top School Log, November 29th, 1940

The bomb in question, later discovered to be a landmine and landing in fields near Bradda Farm, evokes strong feelings among the older villagers. Several interviewees had sharp memories of what they were doing at the time. Ewart Nixon had just been to see relatives when he heard the whoosh, then felt the blast, as he turned into Woodhouse Lane. Jane Doorbar remembers the boom *'nearly shook us out of bed'* when her son was one week old. And Jim Nixon recalls: *'There was a huge crash and fire and soot flew out of the grate.'*

But a brief examination of the School Logs kept by Headmaster Mr Rogers during those years, and the Rev Fletcher's wartime correspondence, leaves us in no doubt that Biddulph Moor had been fully engaged in hostilities many months before that particular German bomber released its cargo. Senior scholars from 'Top' School had already been given lessons on gas warfare, and it had been the Head's responsibility to make sure respirators worked and were fitted correctly.

After the explosion. A boy looks into the crater near Bradda Farm. November, 1940

By May 1940 the whole school had been escorted to the newly-completed shelters behind the Infants (soon to be the Church Hall) and a month later a new cinder path had been laid between the two schools to speed up the journey. (The best time was 3mins 20secs). The Rev Fletcher was meanwhile involved in legal niceties regarding both path and shelter, each of which involved the use of Church Land, and not long afterwards, the use of the Church Hall by the Home Guard - this requisition having implications for the building's insurance.

It wasn't just the Church and school that were affected by War. Evacuees from Manchester, Liverpool and Birmingham began to arrive, their documentation and care arranged by Ailsa Booth. And so did the troops.

The fustian was requisitioned by the War Office to billet British, then American soldiers, while the Miners' Welfare became a temporary home to army officers. The Rev Fletcher set up a snack bar for soldiers in the Church Hall, black-out curtains were installed at Hill Top Church, Mrs Plant of Plant's Yard knitted socks for Lord Montgomery, and both Billy Booth's fuel tanks and the bus garage (where Village News now stands) were acquired for army use. By the end of the War, after the celebratory bonfires had been lit on Bailey's Hill, the 69 local men who had been called to serve were given an envelope containing £4. 6s. 6d and a message wishing them well in the future - the money raised by the Biddulph Moor Homecoming Committee.

Against the backdrop of War, life went on. A senior girl was injured by a falling cupboard whilst clearing the Infant School in preparation for the departure of the Infants to Top School; Miss Reeve retired and Miss Reay married the Headmaster; and the railings separating boys' and girls' yards were taken down for War salvage. Dolly and Jack, Jim Nixon's horses, did their best for the War effort by ploughing his land for cereals; khaki cuffs were stitched by countless local women and returned, boxed, to the shirt factory; the now depleted band carried on playing, and the miners' buses still plied the homeward road in the blackout.

Returning to the explosion. Jim Nixon has lucid memories of the night the bomb landed in one of his fields:

Jim

'We were about to go to bed when there was a huge crash and we dived under the table. We stayed there for two hours until the all clear sounded, then went outside to look around. We found tiles everywhere, windows blown in and doors off. When it got light I went into the fields. Three of the six poultry houses had been smashed to firewood and the hens were scattered all over the place, some dead and the others just dazed. The bomb had landed about 400 yards from the house and blown a crater 30ft deep and 60ft in diameter. The field was like a building site, with clay and soil everywhere. We had to get the remaining poultry houses manageable and crowd the live hens in them while we gathered up the dead fowl. The livestock didn't suffer too badly, but the sheds were damaged, so we made temporary repairs to the roof with tarpaulin.

Later we found out it was a parachute landmine which had been jettisoned by a German bomber. The two parachutes were found about 400 yds away. That was our first experience of war on our doorstep, but from then on we were always aware from the drone of German bombers overhead that it might not be our last.'

INLAND REVENUE,
VALUATION OFFICE.

Telephone
Stoke-on-Trent
48380

District Valuer's Office,
Majestic Chambers,
Campbell Place,
Stoke-on-Trent
Staffs.

26th Decr. 194

Please quote CSW/BP on any reply.

Your reference is..............

Mr.J.E.Nixon,
Bradda Farm,
Biddulph Moor,

Dear Sir,

War Damage, V.O. 323

With reference to your claim dated 12th December 1940, I have to state that after giving the matter careful consideration, I am, without prejudice, prepared to offer an assessment of £10.0.0.

Perhaps you would let me know at your earliest convenience, whether this meets with your acceptance.

Yours faithfully,

District Valuer.

Jim Nixon is offered £10 compensation, war damage.

Reassessment of damage to Bradda Farm requested.

War Damage to Property.
Government Compensation Scheme.

Reference to be quoted in all communications.

District Stoke-on-Trent.

Claim No. 375.

To Mr. J. E. Nixon.
Bradda Farm.
Biddulph Moor.

Valuation Office, Inland Revenue,
Majestic Chambers.
Stoke-on-Trent.
6th February 1941.

Sir,

With reference to your claim dated 12th December 1940, in respect of War Damage to Property, I am directed by the Compensation Board to inform you that it is proposed to assess the damage to which your claim relates in the amounts stated overleaf. You will see that the amounts stated are those which have already been agreed between yourself and this Office. Will you please complete the attached slip and return it to this Office in the enclosed envelope within fourteen days from this date.

District Valuer.

Ewart Nixon remembers the crowds gathered around the crater:

Ewart

'One of the first to get to the scene was Arthur Bailey, then living at David's Bank in Gun Battery Lane. I suppose the plane had been caught in the searchlights on Top Road opposite the Hollands. It might have been making for Rolls Royce at Crewe, Whitfield, the armaments factory at Radway Green or one of the big cities. I believe the parachutes they found were made of Macclesfield silk.'

Fortunately there were no human fatalities. In any event there was nothing the local Air Raid Patrol could have done to prevent what could have been a far more serious outcome had the village, rather than the farmyard, received the impact. By the time the landmine fell, blackout regulations were already being rigorously enforced by the ARP. Hill Top Church windows had been covered in thick card and black-out curtains, Jim Nixon had made felted wooden frames to fit his farmhouse windows and Bob Pass and Billy Booth had blacked out Christ Church so that services could continue.

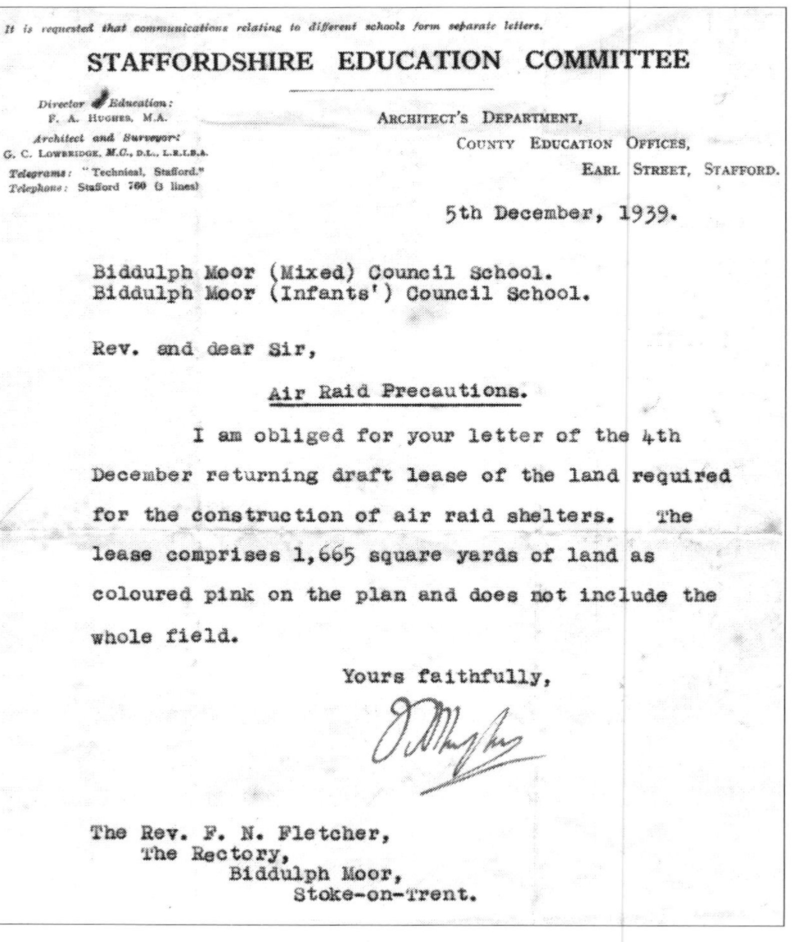

It is requested that communications relating to different schools form separate letters.

STAFFORDSHIRE EDUCATION COMMITTEE

Director of Education:
F. A. Hughes, M.A.
Architect and Surveyor:
G. C. Lowbridge, M.C., D.L., L.R.I.B.A.
Telegrams: "Technical, Stafford."
Telephone: Stafford 760 (3 lines)

Architect's Department,
County Education Offices,
Earl Street, Stafford.

5th December, 1939.

Biddulph Moor (Mixed) Council School.
Biddulph Moor (Infants') Council School.

Rev. and dear Sir,

Air Raid Precautions.

I am obliged for your letter of the 4th December returning draft lease of the land required for the construction of air raid shelters. The lease comprises 1,665 square yards of land as coloured pink on the plan and does not include the whole field.

Yours faithfully,

The Rev. F. N. Fletcher,
The Rectory,
Biddulph Moor,
Stoke-on-Trent.

Air raid shelters are about to be built behind the Infants' School. (Church Hall)

Ewart

'There was a siren at the Miners' Welfare, and Air Raid Wardens paid regular visits to houses which had failed to put up an adequate blackout. They wore their ARP uniforms and took it in turns to patrol the area. Names which spring to mind are Thomas Lancaster, Hugh Proctor and Sam Brown. There was also a Home Guard, with headquarters where Rudyard Road Garage is now. I believe there were other organisations like the Local Defence Volunteers, composed of men who were either too old or too unfit to join up. Young lads jokingly referred to them as the *'Look, duck and vanish outfit'*, but then it wasn't the lads that had to do it.'

Ailsa

'The ARP headquarters was a hut in the gap in the New Street row, opposite what was then the grounds of the Miners' Welfare. There were some female ARP Wardens too, such as May Mellor, Elsie Brown and Edith Holland. I also recall Ernest Mayer. They worked on a district basis, including Biddulph. There were special police, and Billy Booth was a Special too.

I remember I'd been sorting out homes for the evacuees in Kingsfield School and walking back late to Biddulph Moor with Sam Brown and Hugh Proctor. They had their helmets but I didn't have one, since I was spent much of my time in the food office in Biddulph.

During the blackout you couldn't see your hand in front of your face on Biddulph Moor. One night we'd been to a Ladies' Social and we had to guide ourselves to the bus feeling the wall. How the bus driver went on I don't know. Suddenly a wind sprang up and one lady lost her hat. She never found it again.'

Both British and US troops were billeted locally, presumably in preparation for their entry into the European theatre of War. Empty mills in Biddulph, what is now Park Middle School and Fairhaven at Knypersley crossroads were all requisitioned at one time or another, and in Biddulph Moor the fustian and the Miners' Welfare building were taken over by the army.

American accents, until then heard only on film during infrequent trips to Biddulph 'Scratch', became commonplace in the local lanes. The sight of black US soldiers was greeted with disbelief by the villagers, who for the most part had never previously encountered a black face. That didn't put Jane Doorbar's cousins off having a black servicemen to Sunday tea with the family, nor inviting him to sing at Hill Top Church, where he put his rich bass voice to good use.

Ewart

'The fustian billeted the Royal Engineers. The troops made do with the factory while the officers were billeted in the Miners' Welfare. When the Royal Engineers moved out, the Americans moved in. We'd never seen a black man before, and there were quite a few blacks in the US Army.

The Americans were partial to boiled sweets, which they bought from the local shops. I heard they didn't have boiled sweets in the United States.

There must have been 150 servicemen on Biddulph Moor and others in the mills in Biddulph. I suppose there were quite a few liaising with local girls. The one I knew about was Marjorie Proctor, the butcher's sister. She married a soldier who came from London named William Hooper. The marriage lasted until his death quite recently.

The other thing I remember was the harsh 1941 winter. Massive army wagons lined the length of Chapel Lane and were used to keep the lanes free of snow - for the army's benefit, not ours, I suspect.'

Ailsa

'When the fustian was taken over by the army, one of their first tasks was to dig a sewage pipe across the fields to Woodhouse Lane to connect with the works in Biddulph. The Rev Fletcher provided a snack bar for soldiers in the Church Hall, run by local ladies. There were a lot of army manoeuvres, especially along Top Road near the Hollands.'

Bob

The soldiers had a lot to do with us (Bob Pass and Billy Booth) because there was a fuel tank at Booth's and at one time he used to sell petrol. The Americans took over the tank and they used to refuel their vehicles there.

The officers were white and some of the ranks were black. The blacks weren't allowed to go anywhere the whites went. The Rose and Crown was off-limits. We didn't realise how great the divide was in America.

The fustian was just a transit camp to get them acclimatised before going to France. As it got near to D-Day they waterproofed their vehicles and moved south.

I don't remember many ever going to Christ Church, except during parades. They used to store their vehicles around the fustian.'

A field separated Mary Pointon's Gun Battery Lane house from the fustian, and as a small girl she would see the soldiers going about their duties.

Mary

During the War they built temporary toilets and a lean-to cookhouse by the fustian. The US soldiers lacked for nothing. We were playing in the field behind the house once when two of them came up with a sack. In it were chocolates and chewing gum. They also gave us a fruit salad. I was amazed, because I'd never seen a fruit salad before. They gave it to me in a tin with a handle on it and said I had to take the tin back.'

Farming and coal mining continued with renewed vigour during the War years, and the women in Bailey's Shirt Factory were fully employed making khaki shirts for the troops. Further afield, Radway Green, Rolls Royce and Swynnerton needed workers, some of whom came from Biddulph Moor. Supplementary bus services sprang up to take women to their places of employment, among them the Knypersley-based Sutton Brothers.

Elsie Evans, who was employed at the shirt factory when War broke out, now found herself working on aero engines at Rolls Royce in Crewe. There was a daily bus directly to the factory from Biddulph Moor.

Elsie

When the War broke out someone came to see my mother and said I could either go into nursing or the plane factory. I chose planes because it paid more money, but it was very heavy work. I was there until I got married, and when I had a child, after a while they let me go back to the shirt mill.'

Meanwhile, Jim Nixon toiled among the sheaves:

Jim

We soldiered on, ploughing and sowing. It was the first time we'd grown grain on the moor, (1940) because the type of soil and the height of the land made it a poor proposition. But in the War it was compulsory to plough up a percentage of the farm for cereals and potatoes, so as to save on imports from America and Canada. Our crops were not as prolific as in favourable areas like Cheshire, but we did our best under the circumstances. On higher land you wouldn't get more than 25-30 hundredweight of grain to the acre, whereas in Cheshire you could expect 30-40. Also the ripening time on the lowlands was two or three weeks earlier.

Sometimes rats would bolt out from the corn stacks, so we had a couple of Jack Russells handy, and you always tied up your ankles with string to stop the rats running up your trouser legs when they were trying to escape.

Dolly did most of the farm work, but when ploughing had to be done we borrowed my brother-in-law's horse, Jack, to help. We would hitch them together to draw a two horse plough, and when my brother-in-law ploughed his land he borrowed Dolly from us. Ploughing was one of the heaviest jobs on the farm. Other work could be done with one horse.

It was the same when the corn had to be stacked or the threshing machine came around during winter. It needed six or seven helpers to keep the thresher going and each farmer used to muck in with his neighbours to help each other, while housewives bought sandwiches and pies to keep us happy.

In a farming community you were bound to get some black market activities, and whispers that there was an odd ton of cereals going from the more favoured areas often circulated. Bartering between country and townspeople must also have taken place, with meat, butter and petrol changing hands.

Of course, the inspectors were up to all the dodges and came round to check at frequent intervals. He would check on the number of pigs you'd had slaughtered (we were allowed two per year for the household) and make sure you hadn't hidden any about the farm. I'm sure there was many a tin of petrol which escaped their notice!'

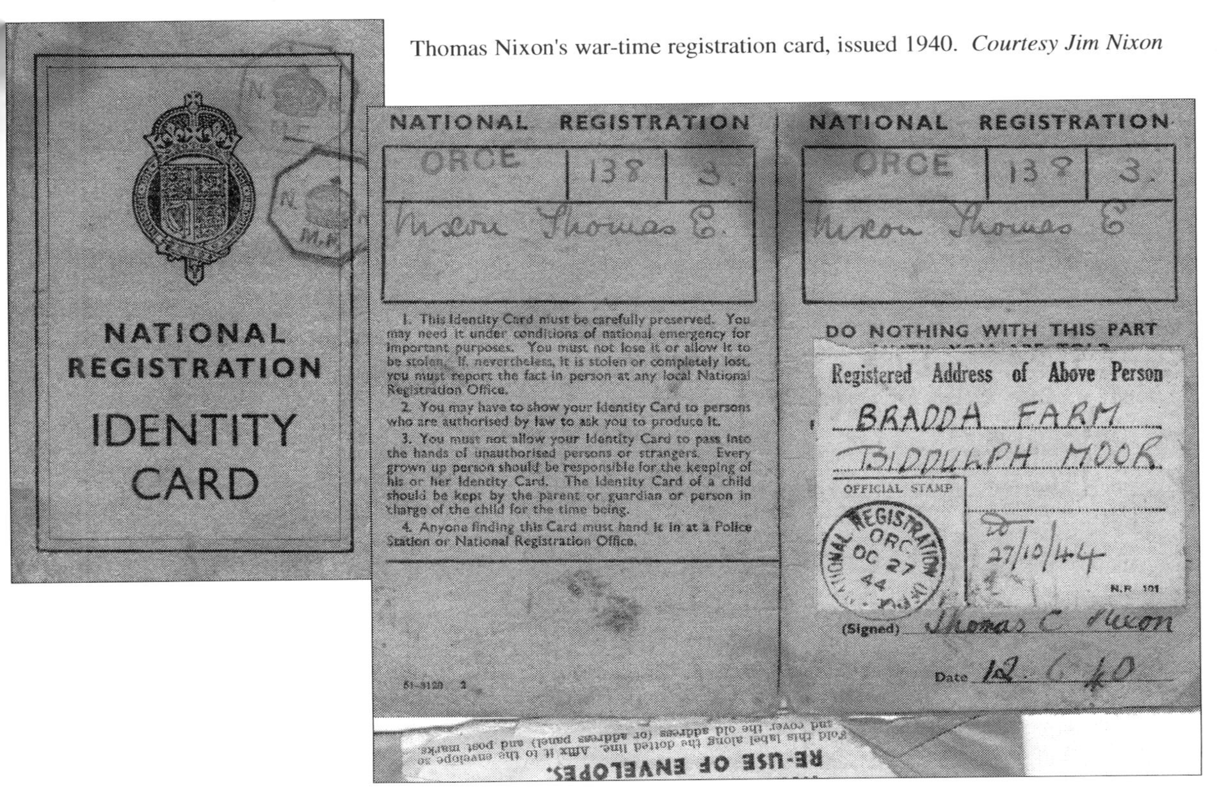
NATIONAL REGISTRATION
IDENTITY CARD

NATIONAL REGISTRATION

ORCE	138	3.

Nixon Thomas E.

1. This Identity Card must be carefully preserved. You may need it under conditions of national emergency for important purposes. You must not lose it or allow it to be stolen. If, nevertheless, it is stolen or completely lost, you must report the fact in person at any local National Registration Office.

2. You may have to show your Identity Card to persons who are authorised by law to ask you to produce it.

3. You must not allow your Identity Card to pass into the hands of unauthorised persons or strangers. Every grown up person should be responsible for the keeping of his or her Identity Card. The Identity Card of a child should be kept by the parent or guardian or person in charge of the child for the time being.

4. Anyone finding this Card must hand it in at a Police Station or National Registration Office.

NATIONAL REGISTRATION

ORCE	138	3.

Nixon Thomas E

DO NOTHING WITH THIS PART

Registered Address of Above Person
BRADDA FARM
BIDDULPH MOOR

OFFICIAL STAMP
NATIONAL REGISTRATION ORC OC 27 44
27/10/44

N.R. 101

(Signed) Thomas C Nixon

Date 12. 6. 40

RE-USE OF ENVELOPES.

Thomas Nixon's war-time registration card, issued 1940. *Courtesy Jim Nixon*

Biddulph Moor was by no means unique in bartering eggs, butter, cheese and milk for fuel and coal. Black market activities were carried out on farms throughout the land, and ensured the survival of those who might otherwise have succumbed to the privations of War. Black marketeers learnt to be especially vigilant, and a case brought against two local bus drivers suspected of being involved in illegal merchandising was dropped.

Despite this, rumours were rife. A ton of oats was said to have been hidden in a hayloft. Full petrol cans were said to have been hidden in hen cotes. Fuel was supposedly swapped for poultry. And an unspecified Cheshire shop owner was reckoned to have exchanged his surplus sugar for a pig, making his homeward journey with the animal hidden in his motorbike sidecar.

However, hearsay did nothing to preclude the more substantive facts of War. Thomas Lawton, George Gibson, Harold Tatton and Sam Allcock never returned from the fighting, while Percy Beech, invalided out of the army, later died. Nearer to home, Mrs Bailey was knocked down by a jeep at Knypersley Crossroads. Her injuries proved fatal.

I choose a final entry from Top School Log to close this chapter, because it provides a snapshot of wartime England in microcosm, related by a Headmaster struggling to retain a sense of order amid the engulfing clouds of chaos. The old certainties might have been toppling, but there were still a few fingers in the dyke - not least Mr Rogers'.

'Workmen arrive to take down the iron railings for war salvage. I have received no authority for their removal. I got into telephone communication with the LEA. The architect's office gave me to understand that the railings could not be saved, so work has proceeded with the railings dividing the playground being the first to go this morning. This makes supervision doubly difficult as there is now no possible way of separating the lavatories, especially in lesson time, and at playtimes boys and girls and infants can freely mix. On two sides of the playground there are pasture fields, so cattle may now wander at liberty in the playgrounds. These things have been pointed out to the salvage authority but to no avail.'
Top School Log, 29th October 1942

William Biddulph, who did not return from the Great War. (See plaque in Christ Church)

INLAND REVENUE Tel. Stoke-on-Trent 4291, 4292 & 4293.

H.M. INSPECTOR OF TAXES

Majestic Court,
South Wolfe Street,
STOKE-ON-TRENT, Staffs.

Please quote in any future correspondence:

Your reference is:

WD.47209/JHR 29th October, 1945

The Rev. F. N. Fletcher,
The Rectory,
Biddulph Moor,
Stoke on Trent.

Dear Sir,

War Damage Contribution on Biddulph Moor School and School House

I regret that your claim to repayment of War Damage has not received earlier attention. Will you, however, let me have the following information:-

(1) It would appear that the school was normally used as an Elementary School, i.e., mainly for educational purposes. Is this correct, please?

(2) If this is correct, will you please state the date on which the use for educational purposes ceased, and the date on which it was used mainly, or exclusively, for religious purposes.

(3) Regarding the School House, please state the use to which this was put during the occupation of the school for:-
(a) educational purposes;
(b) religious purposes.
Was any rent received, or was it occupied by a caretaker, a schoolmistress, etc.?

I would explain that it is necessary to have this information as the amount of relief for charitable purposes varies according to the use to which the premises are put.

Yours faithfully,

The Home Guard used the Church Hall during the war. There was no bomb damage, so what prompted the claim is not known.

'Silent Night. Late 1960s.'

Chapter 8
Ridding the Roads

'My father died in the February of that year. (1947) Billy Booth got the men to rid the roads of snow, and they filled up again in no time. The following day one coffin was taken by sledge to Biddulph Church for burial. Another lady died at Lion's Paw Wood and had to be sledged to Brown Edge Church, the men dragging the sledge with ropes. The lanes were full of drifts, and if you wanted supplies you had to fight your way through.'

Jane Doorbar, describing the 1947 winter on Biddulph Moor

Biddulph Moor winters have long been a topic of conversation among those whose memory conjures up scenes of drifts and desolation, and more than a century of School Logs make constant references to the state of the post-Christmas weather. Such bleak winters seem recently to have abated, and in any event facilities now exist to ensure at least one route into the village is kept open in all but the most severe conditions. It was not always thus, however, and the effect of adverse weather on the local schools alone is worthy of note:

'During the night there has been a very heavy fall of snow with a high wind and drifts in places. No transport is running, and when the Head (Mr Rogers) reached the school after walking three miles through drifts he found seven boys and three girls present, but no other staff and no infants.'

Top School Log: January 1945

'I inspected fifty-seven children this morning, making the journey in strong wind which caused drifts of between four and seven feet deep.'

Nurse Turner, Top School Log: February 1937

'Attendance is very poor because of bad weather, storms and drifts.'

Infant Log, January 1931

'Snow fell deeply, and strong winds caused drifts of up to seven feet deep. The roads were impassable, the bus service suspended. Miss Mountain and Miss Doorbar arrived late and very wet through having to walk through deep snow. Only two children were present. The Rector authorised the closing of the school for the afternoon session.'

Infants' School Log, March 1937

'The school is almost without fuel. Fires were drawn and school closed for the rest of the week. All roads are still blocked.'

Top School Log, February 1940

One of the snowiest winters on record was that of 1947, and Ewart Nixon still remembers the disruption it caused:

Ewart

'Biddulph Moor had a bad time of it. I was working in Biddulph Co-op at the time and I had to walk past Nettlebeds Farm when I was able to get in since the buses could only get up to Rock End.

Sometimes I'd come back from Biddulph Co-op with a pillowcase full of bread for relatives on the moor. When a supply could get through it was baked at Machin's, situated where Somerfields is now. Sometimes bread was left by the buses at Rock End for people to collect.

The old Police Station opposite the Rose and Crown was almost completely covered over. The roads would be ridded and the work un-done by the next fall. Unemployed men were called in to keep a way passable for walkers at least. No milk was delivered, and farm milk was fed back to the animals.'

Jane Doorbar also recalls that time.

Jane

'1980 was a bad winter, with drifting on either side the road, and 1963 was not much better. I was a caretaker then at Sunday School and my sister and I went night and morning for thirteen weeks stoking up the boilers and it never thawed out. But the 1947 winter was the one everyone remembers. When my father died in February the council had to clear the roads manually so we could bury him, and they filled in again that night. The bus only ran to Gutter Lane (now Park Lane) and for three days it couldn't even get as far as that. Quite often the outside services stopped at Biddulph and you had to walk back to the moor.'

Bad winters made farming a doubly hazardous procedure, particularly before the introduction of piped water, when pond ice had to be broken before the animals could drink. Jim Nixon was no stranger to such hardships, and remembers the 1963 winter clearly. Lillian Armitt, on the other hand, recalls her efforts to get to her job as Senior Dining Room Assistant at Top School.

Lillian

'It was hard getting there in the winters, because it snowed a lot then. (1950s) I used to walk from our house over the fields in wellingtons, and sometimes it was over the top of your boots. Quite often the children didn't turn up when it was really bad.'

Malcolm Locker, who taught at the same school, remembers his own struggles to get to work:

Malcolm

'When I first started teaching at Biddulph Moor I had a motorbike, but then I bought a Standard 8 car. Children came from all over, from Top Road, Crowborough, Cowall Moor, Park Lane and further afield. Those who found it hard to get back in the snow were picked up by tractors and farm vehicles.

One year, eight or nine children were left in the school because of the snow. I used to give Mrs Warrender a lift to Rock End and I told her I'd have to take these children back home first before it got any worse.

I set off to drop a couple off at Top Road and Hot Lane, then some at the other end, on the Brown Edge road - and a couple at Crowborough. It was Crowborough where I got stuck and had to be dug out by a local man named Alcock. When I eventually got back to school I found Mrs Warrender had walked home on her own through the drifts.'

The District Nurse fared little better, and Clarice Boon found no cheer in some of the winter visits she made in the course of her work:

Clarice

'Winter could be pretty dire on the moor at times. You had to leave your car and set to and walk. I had a delivery bag with gas and air, but you couldn't carry that with you if you had far to walk. You had to do the best you could. Some of the farms had no running water or electricity, so I used tilly lamps which had to be pumped before you could light them.'

Hard times on Biddulph Moor: snow drifts across Rudyard Road in this view towards Ridgefields. Polly Lovatt's shop in background.

Bob Pass shares Jane Doorbar's memories of winter funerals, when the moorland roads were virtually impassable and improvisation was the order of the day. Working for Billy Booth, the funeral director, could be taxing, but instructive too, as Bob found out one January day during the War:

Bob

Ridding the roads: winter 1947 on the moor.

'In winter the roads weren't gritted. That began to happen after the War. Before that you drove on hard-packed snow. On this occasion we had a funeral at Horton. The dead man was from Congleton, and the only way we could get him to Horton Church was to tow him on a trailer. We couldn't get any of the funeral cars out of the garage because of the snow, you see, but we managed to get hold of this trailer and hitch it to a car which wasn't stuck.

We had to go via North Rode, Bosley and Rushton, and came towards Horton that way. We managed to get him to the bottom of the bank, then strapped the coffin to a sledge we'd brought and dragged him up to the Church on that. There were four of us on the job, and we got there in the end.'

The late Annie Ethel Cook was no stranger to harsh weather,and recalls what happened to her in the winter of 1930 in her reminiscences *My Childhood Memories on the Moor.*

'I was working in Conlowes in Congleton, and this blizzard started one Friday dinner-time. The bus company phoned the mill to tell workers from Biddulph Moor to go home. The bus came to the mill and the driver and conductor had to dig through drifts at Mossley crossroads and managed to get as far as Knypersley so we could walk up Gutter Lane (Park Lane now). To make things worse, there was a young woman who was seven months pregnant and we were all trying to help her.

By the time we got to Robin Hill it was six o'clock and I had to walk down the fields to the farm. I was up to my shoulders in snow and arrived home about seven o'clock. My mother was in such a state. My father had gone to Biddulph as usual with the horse and float for the weekend shopping and he hadn't got back. The cows were not watered or fed, or the milking done. It was a nightmare. My father didn't get back until it was gone midnight.'

'Bleak times ahead.' Let's hope the winter fuel arrived in time.

Chapter 9
Step at a Time

'Most women had their children at home without a professional midwife before World War One, but there was always a local woman who would do the job. One such was Mrs Brown, who lived on a small-holding near Finney's Corner, Over-the-Hill, in the Twenties. If it was milking time she wouldn't come out unless someone looked after the cows. When my father (Joseph Turner) asked her to come and deliver me, she said only if he milked the cows for her. So he did.'

Ailsa Booth, recalling a family anecdote

'My paternal grandma was often called out to deliver a baby. She went in the middle of winter at the age of eighty-four to help deliver a child in a local cottage about 1920. She was told off by my father for doing it in the bad weather. She said, 'I had to go. I couldn't let them down.' Another local 'midwife' went around in a buggy, harnessed to a pony.'

Jane Doorbar, recalling a family anecdote

Lack of a trained midwife wasn't the only hardship in a time of oil-lamps, hand-me-downs, tip-nailed clogs, well-water, long days in the mine and short time at the mill, though what now passes for deprivation was then seen as more a way of life. In fact, Jane Doorbar believes *'People are not as happy as they were. They're more discontent'*.

Whether you agree or not, it's true that illness, particularly childhood illness, was more prevalent before antibiotics became widely available, and the School Logs make as many references to ill-health among the pupils as to severe winter weather. Indeed, seasonal conditions seem to have precipitated an annual toll of coughs and colds, though influenza, measles, scarlet fever and the more serious pneumonia and diphtheria are frequently noted.

Sanitary conditions also left a lot to be desired, the earth closets in the old Infants School yard surviving until the '80s and the first indoor toilets at Top School installed as late as 1962. Such conditions were not confined to Biddulph Moor, of course. Rather, Biddulph Moor reflected the national picture, and accounts of local people killed in mining or road accidents, injured while skating across a Top Road pool or even getting struck by lightning could be replicated almost anywhere. Similarly, criminal activities, as in the rest of rural England between the Wars, were low key, with rare petty theft and an occasional pub brawl among the few incidents to reach the ears of the local constabulary.

The police provided an essential link in developing services to the village, but they were not the only ones. The 'nit-nurse', dentist and doctor paid frequent visits to both the Infants and Top School, and it is sobering to reflect that even during the War Years such medical services were readily available to pupils. And with Post-War developments in health care, the doctor, district nurse and midwife each made their own contribution to the well-being of those living on the moor.

This chapter attempts to chart the growth in such provision, and to shed light on the hardships which rendered it necessary. Jane Doorbar's recollection of Christmas Eve, 1918, is a case in point.

Jane

'I wanted a doll for Christmas, and my parents didn't have much money. It was the end of War (the Great War) and few dolls were being made. Wages were nothing, but my mother got a train from Black Bull Station to Tunstall. She changed to take the Hanley train, since there were no buses then, and she bought a doll for 5/11d from Hanley. On Christmas morning at 4am my sister said: *'Shall I see if he's been?'* I said, *'Yes,'* so she went downstairs and felt under the sheet and said: *'I think you've got a doll. I can feel it.'* So we went back to sleep happy. Nearly ninety years later, I still have the doll.

Life was hard at times then. After the (First) War sugar was rationed, and fat was sought after. If there was fat anywhere, women would scoot after it.'

The deprivation Jane remembers following the end of the First World War continued for some years, and it was not uncommon to find families struggling to make ends meet throughout the 1920s.

Jim

'On this particular farm were a family of eleven children. One thing that sticks in my mind is the mother forever putting patches on trousers or mending socks at night, never having an idle moment. I remember a big range where she used to make huge rice puddings and bread crust puddings in a washing-up bowl to feed the family.'

Ewart Nixon recalls village life a decade later, by which time there had been some material improvement in living standards, but not enough to disregard the cost involved in the purchase of items of clothing and footwear.

Ewart

'Men and women would save up to buy something new for church, like a shirt or blouse. Both girls and boys wore clogs, repaired locally by Messrs Beech, Holdcroft or Gaskill, the latter also making clogs from uppers supplied from elsewhere and wooden soles made by him. Clogs had to be tipped regularly, the tips fixed with tipping nails on the sole. Children weren't allowed out in their best shoes, and were smacked if they ruined their clogs. Tipping was sometimes done by parents at home. For best, men wore a starched collar, which could be cleaned with a rag.'

Clogs were not universally welcomed, as the late Annie Cook recalled in her book *My Childhood Memories on the Moor*: 'Because my brothers wore clogs to school I was expected to do the same. But as I got older, some of my friends didn't wear them, so I used to get up early and take my shoes and hide them in some holly bushes by the side of the path. Then I changed into my shoes and left my clogs in the bushes until I came home from school. I did this for quite a while until I persuaded my mother to allow me to wear shoes.'

Annie's mother may have got Annie off the hook, but it was up to others to extend a helping hand in times of illness. Numerous entries in the School Logs detail common childhood complaints and name ancillaries whose precautionary treatment no doubt helped stem an even greater number of casualties. In 1936 we find a Dr Richardson visiting the then Infants' School and prescribing daily malt and oil to six sickly pupils. Nurse Turner is also a constant school visitor at this time, no doubt keeping an eye open for nits, ringworm, rickets and 'Lack of Cleanliness'. And Mr Whittaker, the dentist, who operated from a trailer parked initially in the Infants School yard, and later date Top School. In the 1931 winter Dr Richardson notes many pupils with coughs and colds, as well as four cases of absenteeism due to pneumonia - all progressing favourably. A year later, Nurse Turner called to put drops in the eyes of children due to be examined by the eye specialist. Dental treatment was provided by a Mr Stafford in the September of that year, when he examined 51 children.

Earlier records tell a similar tale:

21/1/1874 Many children absent with colds and coughs
23/1/1874 Mistress visited the parents of Alice Robinson and found the children all ill with whooping cough

And, during World War Two:

23/12/41 Mumps and other sicknesses have lowered the attendance to 83%
4/12/42 Nurse Turner presented for Cleanliness inspection and advise regarding immunisation. Sanitary inspector called to see what action could be taken regarding the drains
10/3/44 School closes through influenza

Dentists continued to visit Top School well into the 1950s, and Malcolm Locker has clear memories of a typical inspection:

Malcolm

'The dentist would come in a mobile van every so often to inspect pupils' teeth, some of which weren't good. The children were injected and their teeth filled or extracted before they returned to their class. I felt sorry for them, waiting in a queue outside the van. It was like waiting for the guillotine.

Once, the dentist tripped over the mat outside the Staff Room and broke his wrist. The nurse had to be called. I also remember regular visits from the doctor, who used the Staff Room to examine the pupils' breathing with his stethoscope. But in the main the moorland kids were strong, from strong farming stock.'

Ewart Nixon recalls Mr Whittaker, the dentist serving both the Infants School and Top School before the outbreak of World War Two. Pupils from Top School would be taken to the Infants where Mr Whittaker's mobile dentistry was then set up.

Ewart

'You were escorted by some of the older girls. On one occasion I was given dental forms to take home to my parents. I 'conveniently' lost them so I wouldn't have to go.'

Lillian Armitt, the school meals' supervisor and former pupil, recalls visits by the 'nit nurse', Ruth Cartledge, and like other interviewees found it impossible to comment on health matters without at least a passing reference to Top School toilet arrangements during the '50s:

Lillian

'The toilets were not water toilets, just tubs. They were across the yard and men would collect the contents on Fridays and tip it on the fields off Top Road. Before that it was spread in a railed-off area in the school grounds. In the '30s the men had a horse and cart and wore aprons made out of bags. Mr Holdcroft and Mr Chaddock from Biddulph used to sit on the cart eating their sandwiches.'

In fact, it was not until the early '60s, as the school population was expanding to accommodate the influx of new residents, that toilets were finally linked to the main sewer and brought inside the school. The transition from tubs to 'proper' toilets had not been without difficulty, and some of the credit lay with the new Medical Officer of Health for Biddulph, Dr Cannon, who visited the school in the late '50s and was sufficiently shocked to demand, as an interim measure, the use of a septic tank. Anne Newton was seventeen by the time the school was eventually coupled to the main sewer, and Mary Pointon still recalls *'those little wooden seats, with a door at the end of the shed for the men to empty it'* from her wartime schooldays. Jim Nixon, on the other hand, tells of a neighbour who used the 'system' to cultivate prize-sized tomatoes. Jim also remembers night soil operations.

Jim

'One of the night soil men lived at Bradda (Braddow) Cottage. He'd do his rounds about the village around 3am and finish for breakfast between 7 and 8am, which he'd eat on the cart. He went to all the farms in the area and spread the contents of his cart over the fields. He was in his eighties when he died.'

It was not only schools, for much of the village suffered from the lack of drained sewage, particularly outlying farms. Ken Pointon recalls the situation as late as 1950.

Ken

'The council decided the time had come to sewer the village, because everybody up here was on night soil apart from Mary's (his wife-to-be's house). They were posh. They were on a septic tank. There were very few septic tanks here at that time.'

Jane Doorbar, who lives near Rock End, tells a similar tale.

Jane

'When we first came here in 1954 we had to tip waste on our field, as far from the house as possible. I wanted a septic tank, but the surveyor said it wasn't worth it because there'd soon be a sewer up to Biddulph Moor. When the sewer came two years later, it ran up Park Lane and finished at Rock End, and the other sewer ran up Woodhouse Lane and finished

FIRST LIST

ELECTRIC LIGHT IN CHURCH

CONTRIBUTORS

Dr. Lowe
Mr. Knight, Biddulph
" J. Murphy, Loughboro'
" J. Cottrell,
Mrs. Reeve
Miss Reeve
Mrs. C. R. Hall
Mr. C. R. Hall
" R. Hall
" W. Nixon
Mrs. W. Nixon
Mr. E. Nixon
Miss A. Nixon
" S. Lancaster
Mrs. J. Lancaster
Mr. J. Lancaster
" W. E. Fletcher
" F. C. Fletcher
Mrs. F. N. Fletcher
Rev. F. N. Fletcher
Miss N. Beech
" E. Beech
" J. Beech
" M. J. Beech
" E. Beech
Mrs. R. Beech
Mr. W. Beech
" J. Beech, Rock End
Mrs. J. Beech, " "
Miss Mountain

Miss M. A. Brown
Mr. J. W. Brown
" J. Brown
" James Brown
Mrs. J. A. Brown
" J. W. Brown
" R. Brown
" J. Brown
" A. Booth
Mr. A. Booth
" Stewart Booth
" Ronald Booth
" Maurice Booth
Mrs. E. Snape
Miss S. A. Snape
Mr. and Mrs. C. S. Elkin
Mr. M. Lovatt
Mrs. S. M. Lovatt, Rushton
" H. Lovatt
" H. Doorbar
Miss H. Lawton
Mr. T. Lawton
Mr. & Mrs. Wilmot Bailey
Mrs. B. Smith
" F. Smith
Mr. Llewelyn
Miss B. Heath
Mrs. E. Thorley
Miss I. Hodgkinson
" N. Hodgkinson

Mr. G. A. Holdcroft
Miss F. M. Holdcroft
Mr. J. Mayer
" E. Mayer
" E. Yeomans
" & Mrs. E. Yeomans
" W. Pass
Miss E. Boulton
Mr. & Mrs. Harley, Colwyn Bay
Miss B. Barker
Mrs. A. Bailey
" J. Bailey
Miss M. Bailey
Mrs. Barlow
Mr. V. Clewes
Mrs. Shufflebotham
" W. Sutton
" J. Sutton
Miss M. Sutton
" E. Chaddock
Mrs. Chaddock
Mr. W. Cottrell
" Harvey
" Machin
" Austin
" Capewell
" G. Unwin
" D. Brookes
" Bradford
Mrs. J. Holland

No more candles in a jar. Christ Church parishioners sign up for electric light, around 1935.

at Robin Hill, leaving us in the middle without a sewer. We had to fight to get the two connected, and it was 1969 before the job was done.'

Though piped water and electricity supplied much of the village by 1935, sanitary arrangements appear to have lagged twenty years behind - the exception being the fustian sewer, dug by troops during the War. Jim recalls the water situation on local farms before these basic amenities were provided:

Jim

'We had a pump for drinking water, which drew from a 10ft well cut into rock which tapped the Trent headwaters. There were wells and springs all over, with good water filtered through rocks. some used rams, little water wheels which could propel the water from streams to the house. In a farm it was always necessary to have a regular supply. and lighting was either candles or oil lamps.'

Moving anywhere in the dark was a problem before the advent of the dim (and sparse) electric street lamps which appeared before the war, just in time for the blackout.

Jane

'If you went out at night you took a candle in a jam jar. You had to have a long string around the jar so the candle wouldn't burn you.'

Such deprivations were common in rural communities throughout the country, and although improvements gained pace in the '30s, it was to be more that twenty years later that the more outlying properties could enjoy basic amenities. Nor was health provision deficient only in terms of water, electricity and sanitation. Professional care was hard to come by before the War, and although Biddulph GPs covered the area - even setting up a limited surgery for a time in a village shop - they were supplemented by untrained locals who took up the challenge of healthcare with vigour. Nowhere was this more true that in the area of midwifery. However, no matter their lack of qualifications, a former professional District Nurse and midwife, (1951-77) Clarice Boon, is unstinting in her praise of these local women.

Clarice

'When I first started, I was employed by the County Council, then the National Health Service. Before that, nursing and midwifery on Biddulph Moor was in the hands of local women, and very good they were, too. Some were sent for by the undertaker if anyone had to be laid out.'

Clarice's Austin Ruby - later a Morris 1000, then a Volkswagen 'Beetle' - became an increasingly familiar sight in the village and surrounding areas, as the newly-formed National Health Service began to reshape the delivery of care throughout the country:

Clarice

'My job was combined, District Nurse and midwife, and apart from the moor my area included Rudyard and Horton. You had to wear a uniform, a blue dress and white apron, and a navy coat on top. I worked from home. I had a telephone as part of the job and if the doctors needed me they rang me up. The doctors at the time (1950s) were Dr Murphy, Dr Miller and Dr Ferguson. Later, Dr Murphy's son joined the practice.

We used to do about ten visits a day. If there was an emergency call you never knew what time you'd be back. Most babies were born at home. The mothers didn't want to go into hospital.

We were on call night and day. We didn't get too many complications, but if we did we'd send for the 'Flying Squad' - that's what we called the ambulance from the hospitals. If the patient was haemorrhaging they'd come out, and if they were concerned they'd take you back to hospital with them. Some families had as many as seven children, and we didn't encourage mothers to have a baby at home after the fourth for fear of haemorrhage.

Tap water had arrived in the village by 1936.
A few years after this photograph was taken, the ladies' buckets would be hung up.

Conditions could be basic, but you'd visited the patients before and given them a pack which had things in it they might need. As a District Nurse, I visited the elderly and those who were acutely ill and those who'd come out of hospital following an operation. We had to give injections for various things, including diabetes.

Ante-natal visits were paid to the home, so we knew more or less the facilities available and tried to arrange things so everything was there that would be needed. Some houses were basic, but most had a cold tap by then, apart from the more remote farms, where they had to fetch water from the well - in some cases as recently as the 1970s.

We called our kit a bag of tools - scissors, forceps, kidney dishes and drugs. In those days we gave pethidine as a pain killer, and injected it in the hip. Before then it was chloral hydrate.

One of the risks of pregnancy was high blood pressure, and that would sometimes mean going to hospital because it could result in pre-eclampsia, which could bring on fits and be fatal just before giving birth.

On the whole Biddulph Moor people were strong. The miners got free coal, so one room at least was always heated. Some houses had a range where the cooking was done, and bathing in a tin tub in front of the fire was quite common even in the '50s. Clothes washing was done in a corner boiler in the kitchen, with the women either using dolly pegs or a posser, an inverted copper bowl with holes in it fixed to a long handle, a bit like a sink plunger to look at.

I thoroughly enjoyed my time on Biddulph Moor. They were nice people, always pleased to see you.'

So, in common with the rest of the country, Biddulph Moor moved step at a time towards improved health and sanitary provision. Running parallel to this were social developments. The Biddulph Moor Youth Club was founded by Messrs Myatt and Robinson in 1955, the inaugural meeting taking place in the Church Hall; five years later the Greenway Moor Women's Institute was formed, Mrs Warrender, Mrs Brookes, Mrs Ailsa Booth and Mrs Eva Camm the founding members.

The boundary changes which had begun in the 1940s saw Hot Lane, Leek Lane and the northern areas of the village under Horton Parish Council and governed by Leek for rates and services. When the Biddulph Urban District Council took over, a spate of re-naming took place for postal reasons. New Road became Rudyard Road and properties on the road were given numbers instead of names. Houses were built in Farmside Road, Broomfields and Ridgefields. The land next to the Co-op was sold to the Biddulph Urban District Council for elderly people's bungalows. One of the first tenants was Sid 'Times', whose first task on moving in was to remove the glass front from his new coal fire.

By the '60s, Edgar Booth was building in Woodhouse Lane, Chapel Lane and Leek Lane before selling out to Hoskins', while Thomas Nixon, Councillor, bandsman and Chairman of Biddulph Urban District at the time, was erecting houses and bungalows in what became the Parklands.

In bringing this section to a close, it would be remiss of me not to include the role played by the local police in the development of services to the village. No paternalist Victorian could envisage a community lacking a church, and a police presence was usually not far behind. The Normans had established a similar principle 900 years earlier, when their hapless conquests were quelled first by appealing to their fear of an afterlife in hell, and if that didn't work, by brute force - hence cathedrals and castles.

Biddulph Moor was both more modest and less draconian in its pursuit of law and order. Nevertheless, the first police station was built opposite the Rose and Crown in 1896. This was converted to a private dwelling shortly before the War, at which time the police moved their operations to a detached house opposite Hill Top Church, Chapel Lane. This

GREENWAY MOOR WOMEN'S INSTITUTE

(Affiliated to the National Federation of Women's Institutes)

"FOR HOME AND COUNTRY"

Programme 1963-4

PRESIDENT —— MRS. C. WARRENDER
Telephone: Biddulph 2006

Vice-President:
MRS. F. BROOKES

Hon. Secretary:
MRS. J. HOLLAND

Hon. Treasurer:
MRS. R. BOOTH

Assistant Secretary:
MRS. H. NIXON

Press Correspondent:
MRS. J. LEESE

Committee:

Mrs. D. Gallimore
Mrs. H. Camm
Mrs. P. Armitt
Mrs R. Warren
Mrs. E. Davies
Mrs. O. Unwin

Greenway Moor Women's Institute was three years into its stride by the time this diary was produced.

September 17th, 1963

BUSINESS:—

BRING AND BUY SALE and SOCIAL EVENING

Refreshments: Mrs. E. Davies, Mrs. A. Holland, Mrs. G. Swingewood, Mrs. B. Biddulph, Mrs. P. Armitt, Mrs. F. Clowes.

Social Time: Mrs. L. Lancaster, Mrs. A. Gallimore.

Competition: Knitted Tea Cosy or Baked Savoury Flan.

October 15th, 1963

BUSINESS:—

TALK AND DEMONSTRATION ON HOUSE PLANTS AND BULBS
(Stafford Farm Institute)

Competition: Harvest Decoration in Chip Basket.

Refreshments: Mrs. H. Nixon, Mrs. A. Gallimore, Mrs. W. Lancaster, Mrs. Hulme, Mrs. B. Hall, Mrs. J. Brown.

Social Time: Mrs. F. Clowes, Mrs. R. Warren. Cutting the Birthday Cake.

November 19th, 1963

BUSINESS:—

DEMONSTRATION OF COUNTRY DANCING
by Jack Brown (Rugeley)

Refreshments: Mrs. Richardson, Mrs. Holdcroft, Miss Brassington, Mrs. J. Wilshaw, Mrs. W. Wilshaw, Mrs. Clowes.

Social Time: Mrs. N. Wilson, Mrs. H. Nixon.

Competition: A Miniature Christmas Tree on a Cotton Reel.

December 10th, 1963

BUSINESS:—

CHRISTMAS PARTY

Entertainment by Members. Games

Competition: A Christmas Novelty—to cost no more than 2s. 6d.

Refreshments: Buffet by members of Committee.

January 21st, 1964

BUSINESS:—

TALK AND DEMONSTRATION ON SPIRELLA GARMENTS
by Mrs. Unwin

Competition: Old-Time Costume Parade.

Refreshments: Mrs. Harvey, Mrs. Bourne, Mrs. Smith, Mrs. H. Hall, Miss Clewes, Miss Mountford.

Social Time: Mrs. J. Leese, Mrs. A. Beech.

February 18th, 1964

BUSINESS:—

TALK AND DEMONSTRATION—SMALL CAKES
by the Midlands Electricity Board

Refreshments: Mrs. J. Proctor, Mrs. C. Handley, Mrs. A. H. Nixon, Mrs. N. Nichols, Mrs. N. Bailey, Mrs. Beardmore.

Social Time: Mrs. J. Doorbar, Mrs. K. Harvey.

Competition: Dressing a Hat to represent a song title. (Title of song shown with hat.)

BIDDULPH MOOR 1970s

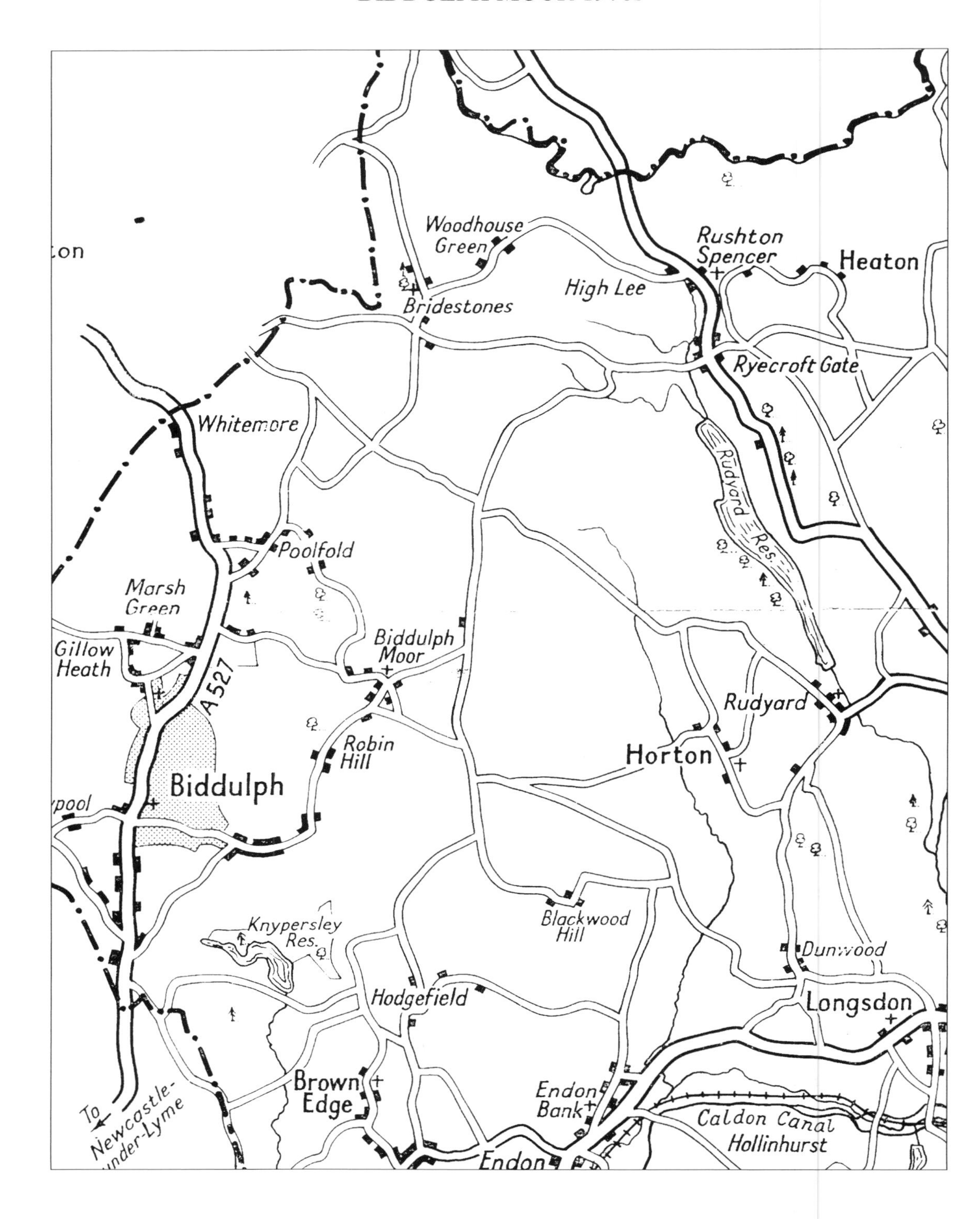

was seen as a temporary measure, and by the early 1950s a large, purpose-built Police House (with a cell) had been erected on land opposite where Londis now stands.

The Police House was in use until the '80s, when, due to another process of rationalisation, it, too, was converted into a private dwelling. Bob Pass recalls the situation in the Chapel Lane Police Station throughout the War years and beyond:

Bob

'Mr Hackett was in charge for a time, followed by Mr Rawlinson, then Mr Cole. There was a cell in the old Police House, and another had been incorporated into the '50s' building. They weren't very often occupied, though. The crime up here was very small. People never used to lock their doors.'

Ailsa Booth agrees.

Ailsa

'The village bobby was a notable person. Everyone knew him. He was more like a friend, really. There was hardly any crime to speak of. He was either on bike or on foot, and his beat was from Rock End to Lask Edge and Top Road to Biddulph Park. He had to get to a check point and contact other local bobbies from Rudyard, Rushton and Brown Edge. The policemen I remember are PCs Beech, Hayward, Hackett, Dakin, James, Rawlinson , Cole and Smith. PC Hayward's sons became professional footballers, playing for Blackpool and Port Vale.'

The occasional wrong-doing did come to light, however, and on 5th July, 1944 Headmaster Rogers was confronted with a problem which, albeit of less moment than the Luftwaffe raid four years previously, caused him to register his concern with PC Dakin. The previous night the school, open due to war-time fire precautions, had been entered. Two shillings in milk money and 10/6d Penny Bank loose cash had been removed from his desk, and Mrs Cartwright had lost 6/6d milk money and 6/- sewing money. Mr Rogers believed the most likely culprit to be an ex-scholar, though whether Mr Dakin pursued this line of inquiry is not known. Nor would PC Arthur Barlow (1949-54) have been acquainted with the case, for by his time on the beat PC Dakin had moved on and PC Rawlinson had assumed duties in the village.

Arthur

'I always wanted to be a policeman. Mr Rogers gave me a good reference when I joined up. Though I was based in the main Police Station at Wharf Road, Biddulph, there was a Section on Biddulph Moor we had to keep in touch with.

One thing I can remember clearly was when Margaret Nixon, who lived on a farm at Biddulph Moor, had an operation for a tumour on the brain in London. We had a 'phone call at 1.30am to get in touch with her mother to say the operation had been a success, so I went up to Biddulph Moor Station to relay the message.

At that time the Biddulph Moor Police Station was opposite Hill Top Chapel, but by the early '50s it had moved to a new place with a cell opposite where Londis is now. That

Biddulph Moor over 60s queue outside the Rose and Crown for their outing to Southport, arranged by the Biddulph Moor Old Folks' Committee. Late 1950s.

carried on into the '70s, and Max Cole was the officer there. Me and Max were very friendly and we used to go into the pub for a drink.

Harry Rawlinson was in the house opposite Hill Top Church. It wasn't built as a police station. He got promoted to police inspector and Max Cole who followed him finished up as chief inspector. It was Max Cole who moved into the new police house.

In the '50s there was very little criminal activity on Biddulph Moor. We all had bikes to get around, and the main office was in Biddulph. There was also a section at Knypersley and one at Biddulph Moor. The man in charge of each section would ring Biddulph to establish his duties for that day. There was a sergeant in charge at Biddulph who would know where each section officer was during the day, so the system worked well. There were five men in Biddulph, one at Knypersley and one at Biddulph Moor.

People were no trouble in my time as a policeman. No trouble at all.'

* * * * *

Doubtless a fuller account of Biddulph Moor awaits writing, particularly its earlier, 19th century roots, which largely lie outside the remit of this book. The history of the local schools and churches alone would repay any work invested in them by the interested observer.

Committing personal reminiscences to print can be a hazardous procedure, and although the contributors and myself have taken great pains to present an accurate picture of village life, memory can be fickle. I trust any lapses have not marred your enjoyment of the book.

Biddulph Moor's third annual outing for old people (which has superseded the tea held for about 20 years) started out from the "Rose and Crown" Inn on Saturday. With 100 old folk on board three buses, they travelled to Southport, where they spent a very happy time and enjoyed a special tea. The outing was arranged by the Biddulph Moor Old Folks Committee (Secretary: Mr. J. T. Shufflebotham) for those over 60 years and widows. The oldest present was 82-years-old Mrs. M. Beech, of Leek-lane End.

The original newspaper caption to the photograph opposite

THE ROLL OF HONOUR & MEMORIAL TABLET, CHRIST CHURCH

THE GREAT WAR
FOR KING AND COUNTRY
ROLL OF HONOUR
BIDDULPH MOOR

Arthur Goodwin
Silas Brown
Joshua Whiston
Jonathan Pyatt
Benjamin Fletcher
James Taylor
James Lancaster
Simeon Battisby
James Gibson
Harry Sutton
James Shufflebotham
Samuel Hulme
Richard Hulme
Ernest Sherratt
Thomas Lancaster
Herbert Wilfred Smith

William Bailey
Richard Bailey
George Hackney
Richard Sutton
Charles Lovatt
Ernest Mayer
James Beech
John Brown
William Beech
George Goldstraw
Thomas Lancaster
Percy William Lovatt
Thomas Wilshaw
William Heath
John Thomas Shufflebotham

GOD SAVE THE KING

IN MEMORY OF THOSE MEMBERS OF THIS PARISH WHO MADE THE SUPREME SACRIFICE IN THE GREAT WAR 1914-1918

Pte. Thomas Lancaster	Jan 15 1916
Pte. John Brown	Sept 8 1916
Corpl. Albert Goldstraw	Nov 3 1916
Pte. Herbert Wilfred Smith	Sept 28 1917
Gunner William Henry Nixon	Oct 13 1917
Pte. William Henry Biddulph	Oct 1918

Author's note:
The lists of those from Biddulph Moor who volunteered to serve in the First World War, and those who made the supreme sacrifice, are taken from the Roll of Honour and Memorial Tablet in Christ Church.
The first list is clearly incomplete - for example local men William and Ernest Rogers are known to have volunteered - because the names of all the deceased do not appear on it.
I have retained both Thomas Lancasters - it is quite probable that two men sharing the same name joined up. I have also retained the spelling Battisby although the more usual spelling is Battersby.

THE ROLL OF HONOUR
BIDDULPH MOOR SERVING MEMBERS H.M.FORCES 1939-1945

SERVICE NUMBER	NAME AND ADDRESS
14561621	T. Ault. Robin Hill, Biddulph Moor
1211345	G. Ault. Robin Hill, Biddulph Moor
7403292	R. Allcock. Stone Hole Cott, Lask Edge
Army	S. Allcock. Gadshill Bank, Lask Edge
14898769	R. Armitt. Rock End, Biddulph Moor
145778882	W. Armitt, Hazel House, Damn Lane, Biddulph Moor
2220499	D. Brookes. Somerdale Farm, Biddulph Moor
Army	H. Brown. 180 Park Lane, Knypersley
Army	J. Bradbury. Rock End, Biddulph Moor
1618752	H. Brassington. Chapel Villa, Lask Edge
7045751	R. Berrisford. Cowall Moor, Lask Edge
R.A.F.	H. Brown. Moor Villas, Biddulph Moor
1640834	D. Beech. Ridgefields, Biddulph Moor
944520	R. Booth. New Road, Biddulph Moor
254281	G. Bailey. Hot Lane, Biddulph Moor
14520726	W. Beech. Radnor Back Lane, Biddulph Moor
5052035	J. Bailey. Springfields Farm, Biddulph Moor
5051031	J. Beech, Church Lane, Biddulph Moor
Army	P. Beech. Moor Villas, Biddulph Moor
14301678	J. Beech. Hill Crest, Biddulph Moor
478326	Kate Bairnes, New Street, Biddulph Moor
13/5057177	S. Bailey. Leek Lane Ends, Biddulph Moor
7362324	N. Clews. Crowborough Road, Lask Edge
Army	V. Clews. Crowborough Road, Lask Edge
PJX220235	S. Clews. Hill Crest, Lask Edge
13054189	K. Clarke. Rock End, Biddulph Moor
1543849	V. Copeland. Nettlebeds Bank, Biddulph Moor
14822672	J. Elkin. Co-op Buildings, Biddulph Moor
F/10672269	T. Fletcher. Ridgefields, Biddulph Moor
14596729	W. Gibson. Rock End, Biddulph Moor
Army	W. Gibson. Rock End, Biddulph Moor
Army	G. Gibson. Woodhouse Lane, Biddulph Moor
7638856	D. Gallimore. Alders Farm, Biddulph Moor
10589122	J. Harvey. Wickenstones Farm, Biddulph Moor
14730458	J. Holland. 280 Park Lane, Knypersley
1823304	P. Hulme. Hot Lane, Biddulph Moor
5040984	R. Lovatt. Sunrise, Biddulph Moor

1173056	D. Lancaster. Rock Glen, Biddulph Moor
14631085	C. Lancaster. Rock Glen, Biddulph Moor
1537267	R. Lovatt. Bank Top, Biddulph Moor
5048298	A. Lancaster. Park Cott. Biddulph Moor
14341763	W. Lancaster. Sprink Road, Biddulph Moor
1966622	F. Leese. Bailey's Hill, Biddulph Moor
1300040	T. Lawton. Spodes Farm, Biddulph Moor
10563376	W. Mellor. Hill Crest, Biddulph Moor
14397609	J. Nixon. Mon Abri, Park Lane, Knypersley
14340261	H. Nixon. Hot Lane, Biddulph Moor
Army	W. Nixon Bailey. Nettlebeds House, Biddulph Moor
14542780	T. Pass. Thorn Tree Farm, Biddulph Moor
4799605	A. Plant. Ridgefields, Biddulph Moor
13054432	J. Procter. Boundry House, Biddulph Moor
165124	W. Rogers. Hot Lane, Biddulph Moor
14683086	B. Rogers. Bailey's Hill, Biddulph Moor
6688765	V. Sutton. Knaylor Bank, Biddulph Moor
2668984	K. Stanway, Robin Hill, Biddulph Moor
2358816	N. Sutton. Rock End Shop, Biddulph Moor
5059019	W. Sherratt. Shop, Park Lane, Knypersley
1710948	P. Sherratt. Shop, Park Lane, Knypersley
2120401	J. Sherratt. Shop, Park Lane, Knypersley
Army	J. Sherratt. Shop, Park Lane, Knypersley
14882849	J. Stonier. Ridgefields, Biddulph Moor
10339997	B. Sherratt. Rose Cottage, Biddulph Moor
RAF	H. Tatton. Kinloss, Ridgefields, Biddulph Moor
11418691	J. Wilshaw. Folly Cotts. Biddulph Moor
861142	B. Wilson. Lask Edge
18155222	E. Worthington. Cowall Meadows, Lask Edge
10534066	R. Williams. Hurst Bank, Biddulph Moor
1502743	E. Whiston. Ridgefields, Biddulph Moor
1090644	W. Webb. Ridgefields, Biddulph Moor

These and the four ex-servicemen below each received a share of the £306. 8s. 6d. that was raised by Home Coming Committee of Biddulph Moor

FOUR EX-SERVICEMEN:
F. GOODWIN. ROBIN HILL
D. LANCASTER. NEW ROAD
J. PARKINSON. BAILEY'S HILL
F. ROWE. CHAPEL HOUSE